MAD BAD AND DANGEROUS

MAD, BAD AND DANGEROUS

THE BOOK OF DRUMMERS' TALES

SPIKE WEBB

JOHN BLAKE

Published by John Blake Publishing Ltd,
3 Bramber Court, 2 Bramber Road,
London W14 9PB, England

www.johnblakepublishing.co.uk

First published in paperback in 2010

ISBN: 978 1 84454 984 9

Briti

A catalogue rec   Library.

Printed in Great Britain by CPI Bookmarque, Croydon CR0 4TD

1 3 5 7 9 10 8 6 4 2

© Text copyright Spike Webb, 2010

Papers used by John Blake Publishing are natural, recyclable
products made from wood grown in sustainable forests.
The manufacturing processes conform to the environmental
regulations of the country of origin.

Every attempt has been made to contact the relevant
copyright-holders, but some were unobtainable. We would be
grateful if the appropriate people could contact us.

To my mother Betty Webb

CONTRIBUTORS

Nick Mason – Pink Floyd
Don Powell – Slade
Andy Burrows – Razorlight, We Are Scientists
Adam Ficek – Babyshambles
Stuart Doughty – Reverend And The Makers
Steve White – Paul Weller, Style Council, Oasis and the rest
Matt Letley – Status Quo
John Coghlan – Status Quo
John Moss – Culture Club, Adam And The Ants, The Damned
Simon Phillips – Toto, The Who and many others
Topper Headon – The Clash
Rat Scabies – The Damned
Rick Buckler – The Jam
Dave Ruffy – The Ruts, Aztec Camera, Waterboys and the rest
Woody – Madness
Gary Powell – The Libertines, Dirty Pretty Things
Ian Mosley – Marillion
Russell Gilbrook – Uriah Heep
Nigel Glockler – Saxon

Steve Grantley – The Alarm, Stiff Little Fingers

Dylan Howe – The Blockheads

Andy Theakstone – Get Cape. Wear Cape. Fly

Steve Dixon – Gary Moore

Tim Goldsmith – Alison Moyet, Bananarama, Tanita Tikaram, Joan Armatrading

John Lingwood – Manfred Mann's Earth Band, Roger Chapman, Company of Snakes

Everett Morton – The Beat

Mark Laff – Generation X

Steve Phypers – The Overtures, The Ordinaries

Bob Henrit – Argent, The Roulettes, The Kinks

Paul Murphy – Elio Pace, Shakin' Stevens, top West End shows

Adrian Macintosh – Humphrey Lyttelton

Pete Baker – Mohair

Eddie Edwards – The Vibrators

Vom Ritchie – Die Toten Hosen, Dr & The Medics

Denise Dufort – Girlschool

Gemma Clarke – The Krak, Babyshambles

Lee Levin – Miami session drummer with Pink, Ricky Martin, Christina Aquilera

Andy Wells – The Slaves, Meat Loaf

Chris Hickey – The Branstons

Mike Wade – The New Seekers

Rob Franks – Badness (Madness tribute)

Ed Sylvester – The Zeds

Rocket Ron – The Northside Jazz Band

CONTENTS

ACKNOWLEDGEMENTS

Special thanks to:

Vaughan Rance, Jane Graham-Maw, Tim Garth, Alan Miles, John Lingwood, Ed Robinson, Heather Anderson, Steve Phypers, Nick Dellow, Malcolm Brown, Paul Kenward, Pete Cain, Matt Sargent, Warren Chapman, Colin Ellesworth, Martin Willis, Hilly Briggs, Cliff Milner, Pete Baker, Ray Fox, Lloyd Gilbert, Andrew Heart, Yvonne Laas, Sara Lord, Alan Glover, Guy Swimer, Malcolm Reed, Dave Williams, Alex Richards, Tom Billington, Mick Brown, Cliff Brown, Mark Sugden, Rina Parmenter, Andrew Mc Crorie-Shand, Peter Lennon, Howard Key, Mace Carnachan and Knox Carnachan.

And very special thanks to my wife, Stephanie, without whose patience this project would have been a good deal more difficult to achieve.

Let's hope I'm given the opportunity to try her patience again...

INTRODUCTION

I was chatting to a mate a few years ago. We're both drummers, so we were comparing notes. Actually, we were having a bit of a moan. Not just about practical stuff, like bass drum beaters flying off and hi-hat stands falling apart, but also complaints of a more general nature. For example, why is it that we drummers are always being told to shut up? Or being made to feel we're in everyone's way?

'Excuse me...'

'Yes?'

'Is that your drum kit?'

'Yes, it is.'

'Well, it's in the way, can you move it?'

Guitarists would never tolerate such rudeness. And don't even think about moving their effects pedals.

We finished our chat/moan and went back to our separate groups of friends. But for the rest of the evening, we couldn't help interrupting each other:

'And another thing...'

Thus, this little collection of drummers' anecdotes was born.

What I hadn't bargained for was the number of drummers who wanted to be part of it. In putting this together I seem to have opened the floodgates to something rather more significant.

Of course, as expected, I've discovered an endless stream of amusing anecdotes. But as well as that, I seem to have touched on sensitive areas which so far had not been properly investigated. For example, are all drummers a little bit mad? Not just the ones who drive Rolls Royces into swimming pools or smash up hotel rooms. All of us. Or do people just think we are?

I've had the opportunity to meet some fascinating people and many of my childhood heroes. And one thing that I've discovered about all drummers: you couldn't meet a nicer bunch...

SECTION 1

ALL RIGHT MATE?

Drummers Are Sound...

Drummers are good blokes. Or good girls. At least, they are always nice to each other. It's a bit like a kind of fraternity. We tend to help each other out. For example, we often share drum sets at live jam sessions. This is partly to do with practicality, as it takes too long to dismantle and erect different drum kits every time someone else takes over. But this sharing procedure also seems to be accompanied by an unspoken, mutual respect. Something which drummers tend to nurture for one another in a much broader sense...

HOME JAMES

One of the founders of Status Quo, John Coghlan played drums on some of the best rock singles of the '70s. His drumming was the backbone of all-time powerhouse greats that filled auditoriums like the Hammersmith Odeon with mops of flying hair and dandruff. It also inspired the famous bikers' headbanging dance. With six hit singles and seven gold albums behind him, John now plays at his leisure with his own band, John Coghlan's Quo.

Unassuming and extremely approachable, this 24-carat rock legend was helping me prop up the bar in his local village pub in the Cotswolds when he recalled a brief incident a few years ago at the famous racetrack at Donington....

The year is 2004 and I've just been watching my mate Nick Mason (drummer with Pink Floyd) racing around the track at Donington. He's a pretty impressive racing driver, that having been a passion of his for many years.

The after-race party is about to start and I am at the bar in the marquee, having set my drum kit up on stage. John Coghlan's Quo are playing tonight, plus an assortment of other notable musicians. Once again, it seems to have fallen to me to do the honours and provide the drum kit, but even though I've never been mad keen to lend the kit out, it's better than all that changing over nonsense.

After a while, Nick comes up for a chat.

'Hi John, how's it going? When's the gig kicking off?'

'About an hour I reckon...'

'I wouldn't mind doing a bit – OK if I use your kit? I know it always seems to be you that gets lumbered...'

'Yeah, no problem...'

I spend the next hour or so mixing with various old musician mates at the bar. Then suddenly Nick taps me on the shoulder.

'Sorry mate, thanks anyway but it looks like I've gotta go!'

'Oh, how come?'

'I'd forgotten it's going to be dark in about half an hour and my driver prefers not to take me home in the dark.'

'OK, no probs! See you next time.'

Nick leaves the marquee and I get back to my mates, but something strikes me as a bit odd. Why would a professional driver have a problem taking Nick home in the dark? Oh, well, it takes all sorts I suppose.

A few minutes later, I'm dying for a piss so I leave the marquee for the Portaloo just across the car park. As I'm crossing the car park, I hear a whirring sound about a hundred yards to my right.

I turn to look. As it's not quite dark yet, I can just make out Nick Mason waving goodbye from the cockpit of his helicopter.

There are, of course, always exceptions to every rule. While most drummers are happy to let others play their kits at jam sessions, the same doesn't usually apply to big shows with support bands, so they supply their own kits. There are occasions, however, when using just one kit can make sense. Usually, whoever is playing last will allow the support drummer to use his kit (perhaps with a changeover of snare drum). In this case the exception proved the rule...

ALL'S FAIR IN ROCK'N'ROLL

Don Powell is the man wielding the sticks on the most widely played Christmas pop record ever, having been the drummer with Slade since they formed in the 1960s as The N'Betweens, before changing their name to Ambrose Slade. Initially a skinhead group, they encouraged their fans to stomp their Dr Martens boots to the music. They soon shortened their name, grew their hair and changed their image to avoid being associated with football hooligans, instead becoming notorious icons of '70s glam rock. They are still touring today. This particular incident occurred back in the '90s.

Imagine. You are a young, starry-eyed kid of 10 or 11 years old. You love pop music and because it's the 20th century, so do your parents. Their favourite band is the '70s glam heroes, Slade. You're really into them, too. In fact, you've got loads of posters of them on your bedroom wall: Noddy Holder and all the rest of the band. Your favourite poster is one of Slade's drummer, Don Powell. That's because your ambition is to be a famous drummer one day. Sometimes, as you look at your second-hand drum kit stacked up in the corner of the room, you wonder what it would be like to be Don Powell of Slade: travelling the world, being on all those hit records, having any drum kit you want with loads of cymbals.

Then, one early evening as you are daydreaming about the glamour of a rock'n'roll lifestyle, you hear a knock on the front door. You hear your mum open the door and there follows a conversation that you can't quite make out, but you can hear whoops and gasps of delighted surprise. You think perhaps your Aunt Helga has paid a surprise visit and you'll have to forget about Slade and rock stardom and go downstairs and be polite.

Instead though, your mum comes upstairs and, poking her head round the bedroom door, says: 'You'd better come downstairs for a minute – there's someone to see you!'

'Who?'

'Don Powell.'

'Don Powell?'

'Yes, Don Powell.'

'Don Powell from Slade?'

'Yes!'

You suddenly feel a little nervous and you ask incredulously: 'W-what does he want?'

'He wants to borrow your drums!'

'What???'

By this time you can hear more footsteps on the stairs and your father's voice talking to someone: 'My favourite was always "Mama We're All Crazee Now".'

All of a sudden, Don Powell is in your bedroom with both your parents. You get up, slightly dazed as he offers to shake your hand.

'Hi, I'm Don. I know it's a bit of a cheek but I need to ask a favour. Can I borrow your drums?' Don looks apologetic. 'I was going to use someone else's kit but they let me down at the last minute!'

Your mum says: 'Of course he doesn't mind! Where's the concert, Don?'

'Just a few blocks away, at the Delta Arena. Do you know it?'

In return for lending Don Powell your drums, you and the whole family are invited to the concert, complete with backstage passes, free posters, T-shirts and CDs. What amazes you is how quickly it all happened. A few hours ago you were lying on your bed wondering what it would be like to be a famous drummer, in particular Don Powell from Slade, and then here you are standing in the hospitality area backstage at a Slade gig, which you've seen for free, with your parents and your sister, talking to Don, Noddy and the rest of the lads. And all because they borrowed your drum kit!

And, of course, you're wondering when you're going to wake up.

PART TWO...

Don Powell of Slade is looking forward to a couple of gigs at a large arena in the Czech Republic. Slade are sharing a two-night bill with an American band currently enjoying a lot of success, as they are responsible for the theme tune to a very big American film. It should be a good night.

Somewhat unusually, the promoters have arranged for him to use the other drummer's kit. Don's OK with that because Slade are on first and he can have the kit set up the way he likes it. Anyway it always makes sense to reduce the changeover time wherever possible and, hey, we're all grown-ups. After all, it's not as if he's going to go mad and destroy the other guy's drums.

So when Don arrives at the arena early afternoon for a soundcheck, he is more than a little surprised to learn that the drummer is not going to let him use his kit. What's more, he's not particularly friendly about it. It's almost like: 'How could you have the audacity to assume you could?'

There's no point in pleading with the guy and, anyway, Don has no desire to do so. However, his own kit is in another country and there's nowhere open within practical distance where you can hire any drums. He is, unbelievably, up there without a paddle, so to speak.

Then someone has an idea.

It turns out that one of the event organisers knows someone with a drum kit who lives round the corner. Don feels a sense of relief, although he still has his doubts as he has no idea what the kit's like and, more importantly, will the person hire it out?

'Don't worry about that,' says the guy in the know. 'He's only a young kid – he'll be chuffed to lend it to you!'

Alarm bells are ringing now because the whole thing seems a bit bizarre. Nevertheless, 10 minutes later Don is walking down the street where the young lad lives, looking for the right house. Suddenly it hits him:

'Hang on! I'm in a band, which has sold millions of records. We've had 16 Top 10 UK hits and toured the world umpteen times. Our Christmas song is the most well known Christmas pop anthem ever. They've been playing it every year for 34 years on every radio station, in every shop, at every party! And here I am a few hours before a capacity gig, walking around trying to borrow a small boy's drum kit?'

Eventually he finds the house and, strangely nervous, knocks on the door. A middle-aged lady answers the door and looks surprised. 'Can I help you?'

'Sorry to intrude on your afternoon but...'

'Don't I know you?'

'I don't think so. I'm Don Powell from Slade, we're playing round the corner tonight...'

'Oh! My God! I don't believe it...'

Then a man, presumably her husband, appears in the hallway:

'Everything OK, Olga?'

'Yes darling. I can't believe it – this is Don Powell from Slade...'

'Well, I never!'

Don explains awkwardly: 'Hello... it's a bit embarrassing really. I've been let down at the venue we're playing tonight and need to borrow a drum kit. I believe your son has one?'

A few minutes later Don is standing in their son's bedroom looking at the drum kit in the corner with a measure of relief because it's not at all bad. What he hadn't known is that the parents have always been huge Slade fans and their son seems to have followed suit because there are Slade posters all over the walls. In particular, there's a huge poster of himself right above the drum kit. Don arranges to have the kit picked up a bit later and invites the whole family to the gig and backstage afterwards.

For Don, what began as a slightly absurd situation has turned out to be a pleasant encounter and a happy reminder of how generous and refreshingly genuine people can be. Unlike the other drummer who wouldn't let him use his precious kit.

During the gig Don takes care to show the utmost respect for the young boy's drums and not play too hard. After all, kids in the Czech Republic don't always have a lot of money to spend on replacement skins.

However, the next night is a different story. The drummer of the American band has been persuaded by the promoters to let Don use his kit. Given the way things have turned out, he decides to give that guy's drums a bit of a bashing. In fact, you could say he has the 'eye of the tiger', because he completely annihilates the kit, which doesn't go down too well – even with the drummer of a supposedly 'rocky' band. But Don figures he had it coming.

And anyway, all's fair in rock n' roll.

Drummers may appear to be an awesome race, but we are, of course, essentially human. And, like all other humans, we are sometimes subject to fatigue and irritability...

NICE TO MEET YOU

Gary Powell was the first drummer with Pete Doherty's band The Libertines. After front man Carl Barât's much-publicised fall out with Doherty, the band split and Barât formed Dirty Pretty Things, taking Gary with him as drummer. Since then they have enjoyed several UK hits, the first of which, 'Bang Bang You're Dead', reached number 5 in the UK singles chart. They've toured extensively and featured at festivals like The Isle of Wight and T in the Park. Gary has also played with The New York Dolls.

I met Gary in a Soho pub for a quick chat and we ended up eating sushi in a Japanese bar just off Leicester Square. It was there he told me about a regrettable incident a few years ago...

It's been a heavy-going couple of weeks of rehearsals, culminating in a performance with the Dirty Pretty Things at the Fuji Festival in Japan. I've just checked into my hotel after a long flight. I've been drinking on the bus for five hours with no sleep all night, so I'm completely knackered and can't wait to get my head down for a couple of hours. My room is on the seventh floor so I get into the packed hotel lift with my luggage and my drumstick/accessories bag slung over my shoulder. As I squeeze in, I am aware that my Vick Firth drumsticks are sticking out of my bag, possibly poking in the face of whoever's standing behind me.

The doors close and the lift begins its slow assent upwards. Then a voice pipes up from behind: 'Ahh! Vick Firth, someone's a drummer!'

Someone's taking the piss. All the tension of the last few days releases itself and I reply: 'Oh Vick Firth, somebody's a WISE ASS!'

The lift stops at the first floor and the doors open. A few people leave and the doors close once again. Unable to resist, I turn round to face my wise ass. Surprisingly, I recognise the face. Then the face speaks: 'Hello, I'm Mitch Mitchell.'

Mitch Mitchell, the drummer in The Jimi Hendrix Experience! Someone Gary has admired ever since he started playing the drums. In fact, he's a genuinely wise guy with whom Gary would have loved to have struck up a conversation, but now wouldn't know where to start. Nice one.

Gary clams up. Well, he can hardly say, 'I'm so sorry, Mitch. If I'd known it was you, I'd have been a lot more friendly because you've been one of my heroes ever since I started playing. Any chance we can start this conversation again with me being nicer?'

So the rest of the journey in the lift is conducted in total silence, with me staring at the lift doors. I can't wait to get out. It seems to take forever to get up to the seventh floor, and the longer it takes, the less appropriate it feels for me to strike up another conversation.

Well, what could he say... 'Anyway, you doing much at the moment?'

Or: 'I'm doing the Fuji Festival. I could get you a back stage pass if you'd like to come along...'

When the lift finally reaches my floor, I step out with a sense of relief. But it doesn't end there. Mitch steps out, too, and then follows me down the long corridor to my room. He's staying in the room opposite!

Not only had Gary blown an opportunity for a quick chat with one of his all-time heroes, they might even have ended up hanging out together for the duration of the hotel stay.

Mitch: 'Great to chat with you, Gary. Say, how about I knock you up in a couple of hours and we can go down to the bar – shoot the breeze!'

Gary: 'Yeah sure, Mitch. Look forward to it!'

Sadly, it was not to be...

Most drummers have their heroes – usually more than one – but rarely do we get the opportunity to bump into them at close quarters. Even more rarely do we find ourselves insulting them in public. So next time I'm going about my business and someone I can't see makes a comment pertaining to drumming, I shall keep my cool and be polite at all times. Just in case it's Charlie Watts.

SECTION 2

YOU'VE GOT TO BE CRAZY

What is it about drummers?

Drumming: one of the oldest forms of communication known to man. That and smoke signals. As such it holds a fascination that sets it apart from other musical instruments. Some would say it's a solid, down-to-earth choice of instrument. You can always rely on someone who plays the drums.

Apparently not. There has long been a kind of universal understanding that drummers are essentially mad. Or if not completely mad, at the very least eccentric. Of course, there are notorious drummers who have in no small measure helped to make this a much-deserved reputation but, that aside, the assumption that the drummer's always the mad one seems to be something that comes from a deeper sense of awe. It's as though the notion is inspired by the drums themselves.

Naturally, all this becomes confused with other influences like over-indulgence in booze and drugs. These are by no means confined to drummers, but nevertheless can have a colossal effect on a drummer's reputation...

MIRROR IN THE DRESSING ROOM

When it comes to drummers from the punk era, Topper Headon is the man. Drafted into The Clash when original drummer Terry Chimes left after recording the first album in 1977, he stayed with the group right through their heyday until his controversial departure in 1982. I met him in his hometown, Dover.

So, the band is The Clash. The venue is a big one, somewhere in Holland. Mick Jones, Paul Simonon and Joe Strummer are crowded round the one mirror in the band's dressing room, taking it in turns to do their make-up and, in particular, their hair. Topper enters the room and asks if he can borrow the mirror. The rest of the band figure he must be in a hurry so they stand aside. Topper walks casually up to the mirror and makes to adjust its positioning. Just as the guys are wondering why he's taking such trouble over his hair on this particular night, Topper lifts the mirror from the wall and places it carefully on the floor. He then produces a bag of white powder, deposits a generous amount onto the mirror surface and snorts it up his nose in seconds flat. He then places the mirror back on the wall, adjusts his hair and leaves the room saying: 'Thanks guys! See you on stage...'

What you might call rock'n'roll. But as Topper will now tell you, that's debatable. The rest of the band certainly held a debate about it, resulting in Topper's eventual parting company with The Clash. It's not that snorting coke was frowned upon by rock musicians in those days; quite the contrary in fact. Certainly, the excessive use of drugs and alcohol as a way to wind up and down from gigs as part of a rock lifestyle was, and for some people still is, totally acceptable.

The problem was that, like many people, Topper found himself spiralling out of control. And that's ever so easy when you're famous, the gigs are huge and the schedule is gruelling. Of course, in the early days it's fun to use a little extra stimulant to ease your way in and out of the proceedings.

Imagine. It's a local pub in London. Call it The Stapleton Arms. You are a drummer in a band about to play a one-hour set on a Friday night. The place is heaving with your own supporters plus a generous sprinkling of pub locals. Your kit is set up and you've just glanced over the set list before taping it to the side of your bass bin. As always at these popular gigs, you're a bit jittery, so you're enjoying a few pints to calm your nerves. It helps to relax you into the right mood – a combination of cool but raring to go.

The gig goes well, the crowd roar their approval and you come off the tiny stage pouring with sweat, just the way you like it. Now you're really wound up and buzzing, so you need to do something to relax. A couple of mates (unpaid roadies) are dismantling your drum kit, so you're free to enjoy a few more drinks and chat with the rest of the band and entourage. This turns into a bit of a party and before you know it, you're back at someone's flat with some takeaways in the small hours (who knows, you might even get your leg over later).

And so it goes with most gigs. At that level it's fine, because you're not playing enough for the partying side of it to really take over your life. You've probably got a day job to hold down to pay the rent, take care of drum repairs and provide you with spending money so you can party after gigs!

The real problems begin when it becomes your job.

As Topper says: 'At first it's great because every gig is an event and a party. Soon drugs are added into the mix. That makes you think you're playing even better but after a while you realise you can't actually play properly unless you've taken drugs. I was on all sorts; cocaine, smack as well as the booze. I'd have to get into a certain state before I played. Then it got to the stage where the drugs were more important than the playing.'

Of course, if you're the official band nutter it doesn't help matters: 'The rest of the band already had their specific image within the band: Paul was the good looking one, Mick was the sensitive songwriter, Joe was the James Dean rebel, which left me with the role of crazy lunatic drug-taking drummer. A role which I lived up to fairly well, I think...'

Nevertheless, being the crazy drummer didn't stop Topper writing the band's biggest hit: 'I arrived one day for a recording session at Electric Ladyland to discover I was the only one there. Nothing unusual about that, the others were always late. I started messing around on the keyboard with a tune I'd had knocking around in my head. I thought it sounded pretty catchy so I recorded it. Then I put a bass line down. Still nobody else had turned up so I put down some guitar parts. By the time the rest of the band arrived I'd got most of the song in the can. Joe went off to the loos to write some lyrics and an hour or so later the song was complete.'

'Rock the Casbah' became The Clash's biggest-selling single, although probably not the most popular with Clash fans. Nobody really knew it was mostly written by the drummer but, hey, he's still living on the royalties to this day.

In 1986, Topper released a solo album for the Mercury label entitled *Waking Up*. It was all about how he had at last kicked his drug habit and the new life he was enjoying after finally getting clean. The public saw it as the record of a man who had won his battle with drugs, having fought his demons for most of the latter part of his drumming career. Not so. Topper had, in fact, recorded the album in order to raise money to buy more drugs. Six months later he was in prison for dealing heroin.

Topper had begun taking drugs to play music. Somewhere down the line, without him even noticing, everything had turned around. Now he was playing music to take drugs. At one stage it got so bad that Topper actually hit the streets, busking and living in hostels for the homeless.

'I remember standing in a queue at a soup kitchen, shuffling towards the counter with my fellow down-and-outs and thinking, "I'm Topper, I was the drummer with The Clash, one of the biggest bands of the '70s and '80s, I played in front of 80,000 people at Victoria Park, I had roadies, I had hotels, I had limos, I had money... and I wrote 'Rock the Casbah'!"'

It's now early autumn 2007, and I'm talking to Topper on a park bench near his home in Dover, where he grew up. He is now completely clean and sober, having completed an 18-month course of chemo-drugs to cure the hepatitis B he had contracted during the drug days. This time he really has kicked it. He still plays drums, when he wants to, not when he feels he has to. And he enjoys it more than ever.

As our chat comes to a close, I touch upon the reputation drummers have for being mad. He feels that, at the end of the day, there has to be some truth in it: 'Think about it. Other would-be musicians opt for something that can produce a melody, something that can give you reasonably pleasant results in a relatively short time as you learn. As a drummer, it takes about a year before you stop sounding dreadful and upsetting people. You really have to persevere at it to become even bearable to listen to. It's aggressive and it's anti-social. Considering the barbaric nature of the instrument, you've got to be a bit different from other people to want to do it for any serious length of time. You've got to be a certain type of person to play the drums.

'You have got to be a bit mad, in fact.'

World-class drummer Steve White, however, takes another viewpoint.

'Mad? No way," says Paul Weller's long-standing stick wielder. "Drumming is the most spiritual, soulful instrument a person can play. Rhythm is part of the very basis of human life. It relates to our heartbeat and our sense of equilibrium.'

Our sanity, in fact?

But there is one drummer who has gone down in history as the definitive madman – someone who spent much of his spare time shocking the media and those around him with outrageous stunts and practical jokes.

NICE GESTURE (PART ONE)

Most people would agree that a book of drummers' stories would not be complete without an inclusion or two from Keith Moon. Mooney was drummer with The Who until his tragic death in 1978, and the most notorious rock 'n' roll prankster of all.

I spoke to one of his peers who knew him personally, Bob Henrit – best known for his work with Argent. We met in The Sun And 13 Cantons pub on the corner of Great Pulteney Street in London's Soho, just around the corner from where Bob's drum shop used to be more than 30 years ago.

I'm sitting in the back of a plane from Rotterdam to Heathrow. My co-travellers among the general public include The Kinks and The Who. We've all been on tour together across the Netherlands.

Tired and relieved to be going home, I recline my seat and look forward to chill out during the flight. But as soon as I shut my eyes, an airhostess arrives at my side with a large brandy: 'Excuse me sir, compliments of Mr Moon.'

I accept and ask the hostess to convey my thanks to Mr Moon, who is seated at the front of the plane, near the portable mini-bar. I look around to see that all the other passengers are similarly enjoying Keith's generosity.

This occurs with increasing frequency during the flight. But no one is complaining. After all, it's a great way to kill time at my fellow drummer's expense.

Time passes a lot more quickly than anticipated and in what seems like no time at all we have landed at Heathrow. I get up, somewhat unsteadily, and stretch my legs as everyone begins to disembark. I am right at the back and last off.

As I reach the door to the steps at the front of the plane, the airhostess greets me: 'Goodbye sir, I hope you enjoyed your flight. Thank you for travelling with British Airways.'

Then a stifled giggle: 'Oh, I nearly forgot – Mr Moon asked me to give you these.' I am now left with no choice but to step down from the plane in full view of everyone, holding a lady's basque, red and black corset and suspenders.

Keith Moon's pranks are legend, as are rock 'n' roll pranks in general. But the difference with Mooney was that he would pay the utmost attention to detail. If a television were to be thrown out of a window, he would go to special lengths to obtain the necessary equipment to ensure that the TV was actually on and broadcasting during its descent.

But televisions, Rolls Royces and swimming pools aside, Moon had a genuine eccentricity which was a fundamental part of his everyday life...

NICE GESTURE (PART TWO)

Bob Henrit recalls another incident involving the celebrated Mr Moon.

It's mid-day Friday. I'm sitting at the bar in my drum store, Henrit's, on Wardour Street in Soho, reflecting on the past week. It's been a long one. Hard work, but business is good. So good I'll have to order some new stock. Bang on cue, I hear the sound of The Who blaring out of the windows of an approaching car. Soon a Rolls-Royce pulls up outside the shop. I go to the door and a voice pipes up from the back of the Roller: 'Dear boy! How about a snifter?'

Soon I'm sitting in the back of the car sipping a large brandy. My host and companion is Keith Moon. It's his weekly visit to the store. When he's not working with The Who, he's here to share a brandy or seven, 12 o'clock sharp.

We discuss music, gossip, this and that. Then Keith says: 'Dear boy, I have something to show you...'

We get out and go round to the back of the car, where his chauffeur opens the huge boot: 'I don't need these any more...'

There must be at least 40 snare drums, laid side by side. I can see at a glance that it's a collection of top names in drums, including Keith's favourite, the Gretsch DRB Special. 'Are they any use to you?'

The problem is, I'm not sure if these are intended as a gift or whether Keith is selling them. But what strikes me as bizarre is how, as a drummer, 40 unused snare drums can no longer be of any use to him. Is he about to retire? Or is his current snare drum supply of such gargantuan proportions that these are simply surplus to requirements? In any case, I'm not entirely comfortable with the situation so I think it best to politely decline, for the time being at least.

Bob never found out where the snare drums came from, or where they ended up. But he did discover that they didn't actually belong to Keith Moon. Nor did the Rolls Royce. In fact, pretty well everything Keith had belonged to The Who. Of course, the band wouldn't have had a problem with Keith riding around in a Rolls Royce and behaving erratically. It was good for publicity. Even when Mooney was not being particularly outrageous, his gestures were always grandiose to the extreme: some people might turn up with four snare drums, but not 40.

But when you think about it, Moon's behaviour captures

the more eccentric slant on a drummer's distinctly different outlook on life. It's about not doing things by halves.

SECTION 3

DANGER

Drummers Beware...

Putting this book together allowed a number of themes to emerge which shed light on what it actually means to be a drummer. In a broader sense, it's not just about the popular suspicion that drummers might be a bit mad. It becomes consistently clearer that mad things happen to drummers. It's as though we are more likely to find ourselves in bizarre or dangerous situations than anyone else...

PAYMENT IN KIND

In his earlier days, before opening his bar/shop, Bob Henrit was the drummer on Unit 4+2's hit 'Concrete and Clay', and played with The Roulettes and Argent before joining The Kinks following Mick Avory's departure in the mid-'80s. He has also played with The Who's Roger Daltrey. Henrit is also famous for inventing the electronic drum set known as 'flats', so called because the drums are literally flat and can be packed away into one, easy-to-carry case.

When I met Bob, he recalled an incident while he was on

tour with The Kinks, playing very large clubs on the East Coast of America.

It's 12.30am and I'm in my dressing room in a big club somewhere in New Jersey. I've just finished a great gig with The Kinks. No one else is around so I simply sit back, towel my sweaty hair and enjoy a cool beer.

However it's not long before my quiet reverie is interrupted by a quick knock on the door. It's the tour manager, Dave Bowen: 'Oh, hi Bob, nice show! You played well tonight!'

'Thanks!'

'Er, where is everyone?'

'I've no idea, I was just...'

'I'm trying to find one of the security guys...'

'I've not seen anyone...'

'You wouldn't do me a favour, would you?'

'What?'

'I'm off to the venue offices to collect the money for the show and settle up with security.'

'But I'm not security, I'm only the drummer!'

'Yeah, but I could do with some moral support.'

I remember that the club is owned by two notorious brothers whose names end in a vowel. Slightly curious and a little nervous, I reluctantly agree to accompany Dave to the offices upstairs. After climbing a couple of flights and walking down a long corridor, we come to the door of the office. Dave knocks.

'Come!'

We enter a large and lavishly decorated office, complete

with leather armchairs and cocktail cabinet. One of the brothers is relaxing with his feet up on his desk. In front of him is a piece of glass with a huge pile of white powder on it. He says: 'Fancy a blow job?'

'P-pardon?'

He gestures magnanimously to a door at the back of the office. 'My brother's in there getting a blow job from one of our girls. You're next in line if you've got some time to spare!'

'Aah, er... how kind. We'll probably leave it for now if you don't mind.'

'No problem! How about a snort anyway?'

'Er... perhaps another time. Actually we've come about the payment for the show.'

'Tell you what, I've had an idea...'

(Oh no, what now?)

'Why don't you take a couple of handfuls of this charlie instead? Call it quits?'

'H-how thoughtful. Erm, the thing is, we also need to pay our security people, who are actually made up of the local constabulary so it might be a bit...'

Thankfully the guy waves his hands in acquiescence, opens a drawer and pulls out a wad of notes. As we leave the office, Dave muses on what would have actually happened had you tried to pay security in cocaine instead of money.

Then I have an idea: why not send them all upstairs for blow jobs and do a runner with the money...?

When Bob told me this story it struck me as a tad cheeky to expect him, in the absence of anyone from security, to accompany the tour manager to see the promoters and ask for the money. It would have been unthinkable to ask a guitarist or singer to go and get the money. The guys might cut up rough and the poor boys might get their fingers broken. But a drummer? Tub-thumpers mate – ten a penny.

SOAK ON THE WATER

Pete Baker's band Mohair toured the USA and Europe as support to the highly successful band Razorlight. In 2009, after 10 years of hard graft, Mohair decided to call it a day, much to the disappointment of their fans. Pete is now doing session gigs with a number of bands up and down the country. He told me of a particularly unnerving gig he did at the tender age of 16 while he was still at school.

I'm travelling to my band's first gig outside my hometown, so it's new territory. The band are all too young to drive, so my parents have kindly agreed to take me and my drums to the venue, which is a converted aircraft hangar just outside Bristol. The gig has been arranged by our 'cool' lab technician in the science department. She wears leathers, rides a Harley and hangs around with bikers. My band's job is to entertain her friends at one of their club gatherings. Although I have been vaguely aware that the proceedings might be a little bohemian, it is only on arrival that I realise exactly what we may have let ourselves in for.

The two-day party has already been in full swing for about 24 hours. As we pull up in the muddy field outside the hangar we are greeted by a dozen or so large, fierce-looking bikers. They are all wearing black. Some are missing a limb, some are toothless. Others are wandering around, pissing

SPIKE WEBB

against the wall of the huge hangar. Most are carrying bottles of booze and smoking what look like huge cigarettes.

So it occurs to me, with some degree of horror, that no matter how tolerant and liberal my parents may be, the folks at this joint might be a little off their radar. Even worse, the arrangement is that my parents are to stick around for the gig and drive me home again afterwards.

As I unload my drums from the car and, helped by the bikers, carry them into the venue, I can't help noticing my parents in deep conversation with Fang, the chief organiser: two people dressed head to toe in Laura Ashley patterns and sandals chatting casually with the toughest-looking bloke I've ever seen.

As I start setting up my drums on the stage, something grabs my attention. At the far end of the vast building is an inflatable swimming pool. Nobody is in the pool and I reckon it must be a bit uninviting. After all, the party has been going on for 24 hours and who knows what could be floating around in it?

Soon it's time to start the set and Fang introduces the band to polite applause. I am pleasantly surprised as all goes very well. The bikers are genuinely enthusiastic as we deliver specially rehearsed, classic biker favourites. At one point, I glance over in the direction of the pool to see a fully naked biker clambering out of it with a bottle of beer in his hand and, dangling between his legs, the biggest dong I have ever seen. It's a little distracting as I'm wondering, 'Are they meant to look like that? What's wrong with mine?'

The gig continues to go well. In fact, it's going down so well that I'm quite looking forward to playing 'Smoke on the Water', which we're saving for an encore. As we approach the end of the set, I notice some strange looks from a few of the bikers. They are pointing to the stage in a kind of conspiracy, as if plotting something.

Tom, our singer, announces the last song. Suddenly his mum dashes to the stage and whispers something to him. It turns out that a plot has been hatched to put the band into the pool at the end of the set. This is indeed bad news. Quite apart from becoming acquainted with the contents of the pool itself, being delivered there by a naked biker is an even bleaker prospect. We decide there is only one thing for it. If we're going in, we're going to put ourselves in: grappling with naked bikers isn't our style. So after the last number, we jump off stage and make a dash for the pool, much to the astonishment of our audience.

We get soaked in water, piss and who knows what else.

The bikers cheer their approval and we come back to play our encore.

Luckily I was playing an instrument independent of the power mains, whereas the others were risking death to play rock 'n' roll.

The truth is, biker gigs are probably the most peaceful of all events. Whatever happens tends to be within a strict code of conduct that renders the proceedings completely harmless, however outrageous they may at first appear. Still, I bet 'Smoke on the Water' never smelled so bad.

ALL PART OF THE SERVICE

Russell Gilbrook is the current drummer with the British prog rock band Uriah Heep. He also features on the UK drum-clinic tour scene, and holds a position at the Brighton Institute of Modern Music. Prior to Uriah Heep, Russell toured with a host of artists including Chris Barber, Alan Price, Van Morrison and skiffle legend Lonnie Donegan.

I met Russell outside Wickford station in Essex. He drove us to a pub nearby, where we chatted for a couple of hours. During our conversation he told me about something that happened back in 1995, when he was on a British tour playing drums for Lonnie Donegan, who was then in his sixties. Russell, I should add, is built like a powerhouse and looks as though he has no concept of fear. He also happens to be a martial arts expert.

We're in this curry house somewhere up North, just me and Lonnie. We're sitting at a small table in the middle. Only two other tables are occupied: a group of 10 boys and girls on one and another table with two couples.

We're sitting minding our own business, tucking into a well-earned curry when I notice something happening between one of the guys on the couples' table and a waiter. Eventually the waiter moves away and I think it must be some kind of minor complaint. Then I notice the same guy gets up and approaches the waiter. His face is red and he looks furious. Then, without any warning, he punches the waiter full in the face. The waiter is knocked out cold.

I'm thinking that must have been one hell of a bad curry when a massive bloke from the table of 10 gets up and slugs the guy who laid out the waiter. Then it really goes off. Suddenly both tables of people are scrapping with each other plus an assortment of waiters. It's a bit like a western because people are getting confused as to who is fighting who. A police woman enters through the front door, takes one look and runs out again.

What is even more worrying is that the fight is progressing towards me and Lonnie. I'm thinking it would be a shame not to finish our curry, but I'm also very aware that Lonnie is not a young man and is, in fact, very frail. So as it spills over to us I decide to warn them away by hitting one of them. Unfortunately this only adds to the confusion and I end up taking on three or four other blokes.

I decide to use a little of my martial arts knowledge to get poor old Lonnie out of the place. Eventually I manage to shield him out of the place and on to the street as police back-up arrives for the female constable and the fight is stopped.

It's another example of how drummers can often have uses that are not necessarily connected with drumming, although it could be said that the exercise involved in playing the drums may contribute to drummers being the fitter members of a band. Russell was not paid any extra for his troubles. He didn't even get to finish his curry. However, later that evening, Lonnie told Russell he wanted him on every tour, even if it was just to play tambourine or washboard.

'And sure enough," Russell added, 'when Lonnie's regular drummer rejoined the band for another tour, I was asked to join on percussion.'

But when it comes to danger, the stage is the place that a drummer really needs to watch his step...

SPIKE WEBB

SPECIAL EFFECTS

Denise Dufort has been drummer with Girlschool since they began back in 1978. They quickly became notorious as the ultimate all-girl heavy rock band, breaking the rules and taking a traditionally all-male environment by storm. Since then they have released three hit singles and 15 albums, touring with a host of heavy rock icons like Motörhead, Deep Purple, Black Sabbath, Uriah Heep, Iron Maiden and Twisted Sister.

I caught up with Denise at her local in Streatham, just before she set off on Motörhead's UK tour in the winter of 2009. During our chat we talked about the difficulties drummers experience with the most elementary pieces of equipment.

We're on a big sound stage at Shepperton Studios doing a dress rehearsal for a major tour. So we've got the whole works: 30 crew operating sound, full stage lighting, follow spots and special effects.

I'm doing the usual, happily bashing hell out of my kit. After a while I can smell something unusual, a bit like burning plastic. I assume it's coming from the stage lights behind the drums. After all, they are very bright and I can feel the heat coming from them. Still, the technicians know what they're doing. They're professionals and this is Shepperton Studios, not some scout hut down the road. So I carry on playing.

Soon I notice what I think must be dry ice coming up around my snare drum. That'll be the special effects guys doing their stuff. Then, to my astonishment, I feel a burning sensation in my butt. It's getting hotter and hotter. I look down and discover to my horror that my drum stool is actually on fire.

Never has someone moved so quickly off a drum riser. I leap up and dive across the stage, whacking my arse to put out any flames. No one else seems to be concerned; in fact they are all in stitches. I'm thinking, 'Hey, guys – I could have died up there!'

Drum seats are generally made of foam padding encased in a plastic or leather outer covering, designed to make the drummer as comfortable as possible. What the technicians hadn't bargained for was the intense heat from the lights working its magic on these constituent parts, resulting in fire. You can't really blame them, because it's a fairly rare occurrence. It's probably never happened before, or since.

But it's also fairly typical that road crew, techies and the like will know every detail of what goes into a guitarist's equipment, what will electrocute him and what will not. But a drum kit, that's just wood and chrome, innit? Anyway, if anyone is going to be seen darting across a stage whacking their arse, it'll be the drummer.

BONJOURNO!

Heavy rock is an integral part of Britain's musical culture, and the band Saxon has to be among the genre's most important ambassadors. The man behind the kit for much of their career is Nigel Glockler. After drumming for Toyah Willcox, Nigel replaced the injured Pete Gill as Saxon's drummer in 1981. In 1987 he took a year's break to play for supergroup GTR, and in 1998 he was forced to take another when a neck and shoulder injury put him under doctor's orders. Nigel was told to put his sticks down for some time, but he continued to write material for Saxon and much of his work is featured on subsequent albums. He has been back with Saxon since 2005.

I met Nigel in The Shakespeare pub opposite London's Victoria station.

It was 1981 and I was really looking forward to my first European tour with Saxon. I'd recently spent a couple of weeks in Italy working with Toyah and now here I was travelling over a beautiful mountain pass in Switzerland – what a life!

The snowfall had been particularly heavy over the mountains in recent days. We had two tour buses, an artic with the PA and lights, and another truck full of our own personal backline gear. The weather conditions meant that we ended up stuck on this road for quite a while during the early hours but we managed to get going and the band, crew and artic eventually got to the Milan gig – a sports arena. The gig had sold out, around 9,000 people.

In those days, the fans would start queuing early in the afternoon. Also present would be a political faction who demanded all the bands play for free, so the Carabinieri would have to keep them under control as they could sometimes riot. For this reason they decided to let the audience into the gig during the afternoon. By the time we eventually got there, late, they were pretty impatient to say the least! The band turned up to find the crew had set up the lights and PA, but there was no sign of our backline gear – no guitars, no drums, no amps! The second truck must have got snowed up somewhere. Our managers wanted to cancel the gig but I seem to remember a gun being pulled so we thought it best to agree to play.

We had no choice but to go on stage using the support band's gear. There was a curtain across the front of the stage, so I had a little time before curtain-up to familiarise myself with this strange drum kit. As I was fiddling about, changing the height of the hi-hat, moving a cymbal here, another one there, stuff started flying over the top of the curtain from angry Italians – coins, all sorts.

I was petrified. Not only did we have to struggle with strange instruments – the kit was totally alien and only had one kick, great for fast double bass tracks like '20,000 Feet' (NOT) – but we had no stage clothes (in the lost truck) to give us any sense of authority over an incensed Italian crowd.

Then something came flying over the curtain and actually sliced the drumhead off one of the rack toms. Even more worrying. Even when our intro music came on, stuff kept coming over the curtain top. By now, gun or no gun, I'd had enough: If one more f***ing thing hits me I'm f***ing off!

At that moment the curtain suddenly went up and I had no choice but to count in the first song after which I got pole-axed on the side of the face by a full can of beer. As the blood ran down my face I figured I couldn't just walk off and leave my pals up there to take the flack. I had no choice but to accept my fate.

Don't ask me how, but we went down a storm!

Another splendid example of how drummers are prepared to get the job done, even in the face of extreme adversity.

UP STICKS

Lee Levin is one of the USA's top session players. He has recorded and toured with numerous artists including Barbra Streisand, Backstreet Boys, Pink, Christina Aguilera, Meat Loaf, the Bee Gees and Ricky Martin. He has also written educational drumming books, videos and CDs including *Drum Programming Basics (Ultimate Beginner Tech Start Series)* (Alfred Publications).

Lee told me about a dodgy incident while he was on a six-month tour of Latin America with Puerto Rican singer Chayanne.

We're in a city in the western part of Venezuela called Merida, where they're known for their fish-flavoured ice cream. Yum.

It's quite near the beginning of the tour and we've made some slight changes to the visual side of things to improve the show. In particular, we've created a new ending so that the final encore now involves Chayanne leaving the stage while the band plays on. Then each member of the group takes it in turn to come to the front of the stage, take a bow and exit. The stage is set up with all sorts of ramps and risers, so each member has to run from their usual place to the front, which takes a good five to seven minutes in total. At the end, I'm left by myself to play a drum solo and then stand up, take a bow, and exit.

On this particular night, just before we take the stage,

Chayanne's manager at the time comes up to me and says: 'As soon as you take your bow, throw your sticks to the audience.' These managers are never short of bright new ideas.

Luckily, I have an endorsement with Pro-Mark and get my sticks for free, otherwise I might have thought twice about it. After about two hours, the show comes to a close, everyone takes their bows, filing off stage as planned and I'm left doing my solo. I finish, take my bow and then it's time to throw my sticks into the audience. But there's a bit of a problem.

My drum riser happens to be 12 feet off the main part of the stage, and flanked by ramps and platforms where Chayanne and various band members and dancers do their thing. This particular venue has a pretty low ceiling so, from my perch, I can almost touch the stage lights. So there's not much room to toss my sticks. I can't lift my arms up and toss them way up high into the crowded void ahead, so instead I decide propel the first one straight down towards the front of the stage, like a baseball pitcher, thus avoiding any of the lights just above me.

Bad move.

The stick hurls end over end towards the first few rows as intended. However, it finally connects with a humungous security guard who has been standing there to protect us. My heart sinks as it pelts him right between the eyes.

He doesn't look at all pleased. I throw the second stick aimlessly up in the air and bolt off stage as fast as I can.

About ten minutes later I'm downing some water and walking back to the dressing room, thinking I'd got away with assaulting a huge tough guy whose job it is to look after the likes of me. Then I hear a door slam at the end of the corridor behind me. I turn and there he is, running towards me. He looks furious and has a large red welt on his brow. And he's big, very big. What's more, he's holding the offending stick, so there's no doubt as to the purpose of his mission. I'm shaking and thinking to myself, 'I don't want to die in Venezuela!'

As he approaches I resign myself to whatever's coming. Then all of a sudden I am overwhelmed with relief as the guy grabs my hand, shakes it with a big smile, and asks me to sign the stick. Still shaking, I sign the stick and apologise for maiming him. He thanks me and strolls off like a true gentle giant.

Later in the dressing room I realise I've learned an important lesson: never throw a sharp object overhand at someone unless you want to hurt them.'

Lee was lucky. These security guards are not particularly well trained in the art of forgiveness, especially not when it comes to cheeky drummers. Lee told me he had tossed many sticks to many audiences after that day, but every single one had left his palm softly and with an exaggerated underhand motion. A lot less dramatic, but a good deal safer.

ROADIES

Roadies. That's what we used to call them. We didn't have drum techs, guitar techs, on-stage fold-back mixing engineers, lighting crew or special effects people. Just roadies. And they did everything, for nothing. When I was in Sid Sideboard And The Chairs, we used to joke that our roadies were to be paid

£5 a year – but they had to work a year in hand before payment. When we split up we actually gave our last remaining roadie a fiver – a year later.

The point is, when you're young and famous in your local town, friends who don't actually play anything are still keen to be involved, especially if it looks as though you might be heading for the big time. Moreover, there was a genuine sense of camaraderie and a kind of passion about the whole thing. The band had taken on the essence of a worthwhile cause. These roadies knew that, in reality, if we became successful they wouldn't be coming with us. But that wasn't the point. These were people who really felt we deserved to make it.

So it was that for some four years a collection of faithful, unpaid mates humped gear, drove vans, set up drums (thank you Neil!), repaired drums (thanks again Neil!), mended amplifiers, put up second-hand lighting rigs and set off fireworks (special effects).

These friends of ours were actually very good at achieving what they did, given the limited resources at their disposal (with the exception of a BBC Dalek that kept poking me in the back during a gig at Watford College – where did they get that from?). However, not everything always went according to plan...

The Queens Arms, Harrow, Middlesex, Saturday night sometime in 1978. Sid Sideboard And The Chairs are due to play to a crowd of locals plus some home-grown fans of our own. The pub features a long bar along the back wall of a good-sized main room. Upholstered seats and occasional tables are positioned around the room and a small dance area has been cleared near the front of the stage, which is small and compact, as they always are when an establishment is first and foremost a pub and is transformed into a venue at weekends.

We haven't played here before, but are here on request of the landlord, who has heard that we put on a bit of a spectacle and attract a good crowd. He reckons he can clean up behind the bar. So he's laid on extra bar staff to meet the demand. We, or rather our roadies, have set up and the band and entourage are sitting at a couple of tables at the front, near the side entrance.

People are drifting in through the main entrance to the bar and it looks like it's going to be a busy night. I glance at the various toys and props laid out at the side of the stage and notice a strange round object with a lead attached, which is trailing off to some hidden plug behind the stage. I ask one of our roadies, Charlie, what it is and he tells me it's a new special effect and I'll have to wait and see. It's not unusual to see various mechanical or electrical contraptions lying around for which there seems to be little explanation, and as I'm not the most practical of people, the boys generally think it's best to keep me away from that side of things. So I think nothing of it.

Around 9pm we take the stage to some applause and begin our set. There's a small line of fairly primitive disco lights at the front of the stage, facing the band. They are flashing in a sequence of colours and combined with a couple of house spot lights trained on us from above, we've got a bit of stage atmosphere.

Towards the middle of our set, I notice that smoke is drifting onto the stage from the front. It begins to swirl around the amps and speakers, then my drums. Soon it begins to rise and the smell becomes more pungent and intense. However, we continue playing in the belief that the people responsible for this special effect will have it all under control.

Not so. As we play on, the smoke continues to rise so that the stage becomes a white haze and I begin to cough almost uncontrollably – not good when you are supposed to be delivering tight, reliable drumming. By now, even though they are only a few feet away, I am unable to see other members of the band. I can just make out their outlines through the smoke.

Eventually we finish the song, and there is complete silence. Not one solitary clap. Then we hear the sound of fire engines approaching. Someone opens the side door near the stage and the smoke begins to clear. As we assemble at the front of the stage, the smoke clears to reveal a deserted function room – except for one person, the landlord, who is standing behind the bar with an expression of anger and disbelief.

Someone from across the road has seen people climbing out of the pub windows as smoke billowed from the building and, naturally assuming the worst, called the fire brigade. After a series of explanations the firemen leave, satisfied that there is no fire. The landlord, on the other hand, is not at all satisfied about the way things have turned out and is definitely not impressed with our special effects team. Needless to say, we are not paid.

It turned out that the circular object I had spied earlier was a homemade smoke machine that generated real smoke. It was in essence an electric hotplate on which had been placed a kind of gunpowder designed for use as a smoke screen during World War 1. (Where on earth did they get this?) It had been switched on for effect, but was far more powerful than anticipated and, as the smoke rapidly filled the room, the person responsible for the device realised he didn't know how to turn it off. Switching it off at the mains proved impossible because no one could find the plug socket in the thick smoke.

This particular gig was the first of two booked for consecutive weekends at this pub, so we were due to go back and play again the next Saturday night. Whether through naivety or sheer arrogance, we actually had the audacity to turn up. Not surprisingly, our second visit turned out to be a short one. As we sat having a beer waiting for the roadies to unload, the landlord approached us, accompanied by a huge, vicious Rottweiler. He told us to leave immediately and never return. In the van on the way back to our local pub, I politely suggested dry ice might be better next time.

Charlie said we couldn't afford it. He'd have to modify the hotplate.

AN UNFORGETTABLE FINALE

Andy Wells, or Wellsy as he is better known, is the drummer with popular covers band The Slaves. In the early '80s he played for Meat Loaf and, after that, Then Jericho and Romeo's Daughter. Andy has also featured in videos and on TV with Roxette and John Parr. As well as committing to a busy gigging schedule with The Slaves, he and the band also compose library music.

This story takes us back to the 1980s, when Wellsy is drumming for the mighty Meat Loaf at a big gig somewhere on the island of Jersey.

The place is heaving, 10,000 people or more. We're about half way through the set and the crowd are pretty wild. Suddenly, the manager of the venue comes on stage looking very serious. He stops the band and announces over the mike that there has been an IRA bomb alert and we all have to leave immediately. The entire venue is evacuated and we hang around chewing the fat while it is thoroughly searched.

'Shame, that was going well…'

'Yeah, I was looking forward to really giving it some on 'Bat Out of Hell'.'

'Trouble is, you lose momentum when something like this happens…'

'Ah well, at least we've got the rest of the night to party somewhere…'

Then someone comes up and says the place is clear and it's all on again. Some bright spark has decided to drag all 10,000 people back in for the rest of the show. We get back on stage and plough back into the set. As it happens, we seem to get a real rush of energy from the re-instated crowd and far from losing momentum, we actually gain it. Everyone's up for it. Eventually we get to our last song, 'Bat Out of Hell'.

The band give it their all, Meat really is giving it hell and I'm sweating buckets after hours of mental pounding. And I've kind of forgotten all about the bomb scare. We finish the song with an almighty crescendo. Then it happens.

There is this massive explosion. Big white lights and smoke everywhere. Of course, I think it's the bomb, and it scares me big time. I'm all at once shocked and terrified.

After a while, I realise it's the result of the special effects pyrotechnics team being a little over zealous. But my sense of relief has arrived a little too late and I fear for my drum tech, who I suspect will have some extra drum stool cleaning to do in due course.

Ah yes, fear can have particularly unpleasant physical consequences... Drum tech? Nice work if you can get it.

STAGE FRIGHT

One of the few bands from the punk era to have carried on playing without breaking up or re-forming is The Vibrators. Eddie Edwards has been their drummer from day one when Knox Carnachan put the band together back in the mid-'70s. He still tours with them all over Europe.

Eddie sent me some on-stage experiences that illustrate how dangerous a game drumming can be.

The Vibrators are headlining at a punk festival back in the '70s. It's the height of the punk era, the bands are attracting huge crowds, and tonight is a packed show. I am on a big drum riser at the back of the stage so I've got a great view of the crowd, who are going crazy as we approach the climax of our set. It's that moment I always anticipate with excitement: the final crescendo at the end of the last number when I give it everything I've got to create that ultimate dramatic ending to the gig.

I leap up in the air to deliver that final crash on the cymbals. Then it happens. I feel the force of an incredible blow to the head. My vision goes blank as I begin to stagger. As I put my hand to my face and as my sight returns I realise that what I thought to be pure sweat is in fact blood.

But it doesn't end there. Suddenly, the stage lights go to a blackout. I take one step backwards and find myself falling in limbo for what seems like ages. A brief thought rushes into my damaged head: 'Ah well! If it's my time I guess this isn't such a bad way to go...' And then I hit the ground. As a well of relief rises from within, I realise that I have survived with just cuts and bruises.

Of course, on these occasions it's important to establish what has actually happened. It's not long before I discover that I have smashed my head on the bottom corner of the giant red 'V' that had been erected above the drum riser. No consideration had been given to the fact that, as a drummer in a punk band, I might indulge in some flamboyant behaviour. Not only that, my drum riser had been set up right at the very back of the stage, behind which is a drop of 20 feet. There was only a gap of six inches between myself and the dark abyss behind. So even if I were not disposed to dramatic leaps but chose to leave the stage with a cool, casual countenance, I would still have plunged into oblivion.

Just to make absolutely sure I had no chance of escape, the lighting guys went for a dramatic blackout just as I was at the point where I was likely to need as much light as possible to avoid that 20-foot drop.

Put the drummer up on a riser. It's a great way to show his kit off and get him out of the way. Just measure up the outer dimensions of the drum set and Bob's your uncle. Then bung it all right up the back where all the colourful dangly bits are. Anyway, Eddie only needed four stitches – nothing to whinge about.

Hastily erected stages made out of chipboard are another excellent arena for musicians to behave like Charlie Chaplin. Eddie remembers one such stage at a festival in Libourne, France.

During our set, our heroic guitarist, John Ellis, leapt from the drum riser – as you do – and disappeared from my view. I figured he was lying on his back and giving it his all in true rock 'n' roll style. But for some reason all I could see was hundreds of people convulsed with laughter. All became clear a few seconds later as helpers ran on to pull John out of a huge hole in the stage. Lucky for him it was just scratches and bruises and a chunk out of his Gibson. Needless to say, the rest of the set was devoid of acrobatics. In fact, Knox and the boys were walking on egg shells.

More embarrassing for me was a show at Middlesbrough Rock Garden, where an extension had been built on the front of the stage. Our encore at the time was 'Troops of Tomorrow', which starts with a mournful tom-tom beat on the drums and slowly builds to its climax. The cool thing was for me to walk on alone and start with the others following on gradually. But being a big-headed git I figured I could hog the limelight for a few seconds by going to the front of the stage and announcing the song. So I walk out so cooool that James Dean would look a nerd next to me.

Shame I forgot the lip at the front of the stage. I tripped over it, head-butted the microphone, plunged over the monitor and fell head first into the crowd, closely followed by the mic stand and monitor, and lay in a crumpled heap on the floor.

The crowd were falling about laughing so much they couldn't help me. I had to struggle to my feet on my own, replace the monitor and mic stand and clamber back on stage to even more laughter and jeers from the crowd, even as the other guys were coming on stage giggling and smirking at my oafishness. Of course, I had no choice but to see the funny side but I was relieved to get back behind my kit.

At the end of the day, the drummer's always the fall guy. Yes, it can be hazardous up there. Dylan Howe from The Blockheads has been there too...

Misjudging the height of a stage even by the tiniest amount can prove unforgettably painful. I discovered this at the Borderline venue in the West End of London. I was doing a gig with the excellent Canadian guitarist Tony Smith during one of drummer Neil Conti's club nights in the mid-'90s. The house was full and we were assembling on the side of the stage after a good soundcheck and I was really proud to be taking the stage with these guys. Everything seemed just right and I was feeling full of energy.

As the rest of the guys started plugging in, instead of just carefully mounting the stage, I thought I'd go for gold – take a run up and jump it. Unfortunately, when I was halfway airborne my shin connected with the sheer steel edge of the stage. Arriving on the stage on your face with a throbbing shin is not ideal.

I immediately stood up, acted like nothing was wrong and tried to hobble round to enter the kit hi-hat side. It wasn't until I had sat down and started rubbing my shin that that I noticed I now had a small red waterfall appearing through my jeans and my right leg was in an uncontrollable spasm. With the rest of the guys still sensitively enquiring whether I was OK, and with tears running down my face, I said, 'Yeah, of course!' It wasn't until the end of the fourth song that my bass drum foot had stopped having an erratic mind of its own.

So we've seen how explosions, smoke, dodgy stages and the fact that drum risers are never big enough can all be a source of danger, but there are other risks involved in being a drummer. One of those is the fact that you are the one instrument that often acts as the unofficial conductor, and as such you are responsible for the general smooth running of things. If it goes wrong, you risk looking a complete idiot…

EVERYONE LOVES A BIG ENDING

John Lingwood is a personal friend, perhaps best known as a member of Manfred Mann's Earth Band from 1979 to 1987. He featured on the albums *Chance*, *Somewhere in Africa*, *Budapest Live*, *Criminal Tango* and *Masque*. Between 1998 and 2002, John played with Company of Snakes, largely made up of ex-members of Whitesnake. He has also spent many years touring with Roger Chapman from '70s blues-rock band Family.

John told me about a particularly scary performance back in the early '80s, when he was playing drums in the then-longest running musical of all at a major London theatre.

I'm drumming in a hugely popular West End musical, renowned as the author's best work yet. It's hard work, as my concentration has to be spot on. I always look forward to the last song as I can relax into a dramatic ending, which is always fun and rewarding. So far each performance has been a roaring success.

Tonight the writer and composer of the musical is in the house. To mark the occasion a special encore has been planned for the end of the show, a reprise of some musical high points followed by a rousing finale. To put the icing on the cake, the much-celebrated writer of the musical has agreed to wow the crowd by taking the stage to conduct the finale.

So we get to the end of the show. Usually the crowd applauds enthusiastically, but tonight there are cries for more and we begin the encore to ecstatic cheers. Right on cue, the celebrated composer walks on stage. There is rapturous applause. The effect is electrifying. I can feel the anticipation of musicians and audience alike as the band begins the chorus of the last song in the medley. Then we hit the last coda which is prolonged into organised chaos for a truly dramatic finish on the last note.

Bliss. This is the moment I've been waiting for. All the hard work and concentration is behind me. Nothing can go wrong now. The audience are applauding already. Someone stands up in the front row. Then others follow suit. Soon the whole place is standing.

I am shimmering my cymbals in a frenzy for maximum dramatic effect. I continue until it feels right for the show to end with a final stroke from the whole band. I look up in anticipation for the writer-turned-conductor to signify that final stroke, but the man with the baton looks back at me with a worried expression. What could be wrong? There's nothing left to go wrong!

So I carry on, waiting for a sign. But nothing happens. He just looks increasingly more distressed. Panic ensues. The violinists are looking pleadingly at the man with the baton as their arms begin to ache with the strain of frantic random bowing. Cellists glance at each other in alarm. Even the audience look confused. Heads turn in all directions, looking for some kind of sign as to when the music's actually going to stop. Suddenly everyone turns to look at me.

I have a choice. I can wait for the conductor to do something, which is what I'm supposed to do, or I risk everything and take the law into my own hands. Oh well, here goes. I deliver a loud, slow roll round my tom toms to signify where the last stroke of the conductor's baton should be. Luckily, it works and the piece actually finishes reasonably well. I can't believe the look of relief on the conductor's face.

Later, we are both leaving the building via the backstage door to visit the pub opposite. He turns to me: 'Thanks for that.'

I tell him I'd like a pint of Guinness.

It's the stuff of nightmares: no one seems to know when to stop or how to end the piece. The truth is the conductor, not being a real conductor, had no idea how to signify such an ending with his baton. So once again it's down to the drummer to take hold of the situation and, in a split second, pull a happy ending out of the bag.

But make no mistake – if it hadn't worked, the whole unfortunate business would have been John's fault.

SECTION 4

MONSTROUS BEHAVIOUR

You don't have to be mad to be a punk drummer, but it helps...

I've been lucky enough to interview some top-drawer drummers from the punk era, a cultural explosion that fully embraced the concept of madness as inspired by a kind of social and musical anarchy. As you might expect, these gentlemen are able to recall numerous occasions when they have either been the instigators or recipients of bizarre and outrageous behaviour...

OUTRAGEOUS

In the scruffy west London suburb of Brentford there's a pub called The Griffin. One quiet mid-afternoon found me pushing on its heavy front door and as it opened with a long squeak, several bar flies gave me the once over. As I looked around furtively, one young girl asked: 'Are you looking for Rat?'

'Y-yes actually I am... How did you know?'

'Anyone who comes in here like that is usually looking for Rat.'

It turned out that the young girl was his daughter. Apparently Rat was on his way to meet me. I order a Guinness and wait.

Rat Scabies (real name Chris Miller) was the drummer with the punk band The Damned from 1975 to 1996. He claimed to be the 'fastest drummer in punk' and was particularly well known for setting fire to his kit at the end of a gig. Since leaving The Damned he has played with various outfits. However, in 2005 he reinvented himself as an intrepid explorer with the publication of his book (with music journalist Christopher Dawes) *Rat Scabies and the Holy Grail*, in which he hunts for treasure in the French Pyrenees.

When I phoned Rat, at first he seemed a little suspicious of who I was and what I was doing. Well, to be fair, I could be any old nutter invading his privacy, trying to get a story. In fact, you could say he was spot on. When I explained I was putting together a book of drummers' stories and that I was currently interviewing famous people from the punk era, he said in a deep and mischievous voice: 'I hope you know what you're letting yourself in for, Spike...'

When I eventually caught up with him at his local in Brentford (where he is still known as Rat) I discovered him to be a very affable fellow. Over a couple of pints of Guinness he told me a whole bunch of stuff. I particularly liked hearing about a brief Damned reunion on TV.

LWT were doing a show about the diverse musical decade that was the '70s, called *The Trouble With The '70s*. The predominant feature throughout this broadcast was the effect of punk and all the mayhem associated with its culture. The producer of the show was a polite, softly spoken lady who remembered punk rock with a certain amount of awe and had decided that, to finish the show, it would be great to feature a performance by The Damned who, featuring Captain Sensible in their ranks, were notorious for being particularly outrageous.

The Damned agreed to play, or rather mime, and duly assembled at the LWT studios for the live broadcast. The producer had an idea that she felt might be a nice, elaborate way to finish the show, so she grabbed the drummer of The Damned for a brief discussion.

'Hello, you must be Rat!'

'Yep, that's me!'

'Ah, pleased to meet you. I was wondering, when The Damned have finished the song, could you possibly smash up the drums?'

'I'm afraid that might be a bit difficult.'

'Oh. Why's that?'

'Well, we're miming, you see, and it wouldn't really work because there would be no sound to go with the drums being smashed up at random. It would look a bit silly.'

'Oh, that's a shame…'

'I tell you what, though. If you like, I could set fire to the drums instead…'

'Oh! Super!'

So Rat had a word with his roadie/drum tech, who was well used to this kind of lark as he had been providing lighter fuel for exactly the same purpose since in the '70s. He went off to find some. In fact, he was a little over-zealous and returned with several plastic baby bottles full of the stuff.

In the meantime the fire department had been informed about the plans but on seeing the happy roadie with his bottles of fuel, they decided to implement a safety measure. They give Rat a code word which he had to shout out in the event that anything got out of hand.

So the show was recorded and the time came for The Damned to take to the stage for the grand finale. Rat pretended to pound the drums (an APK kit provided by Premier) until the time came to light the fuel, which had been liberally poured over the drums just at the right moment.

What happend next surprised even the roadie. The flames created by the whoosh of the explosion immediately reached up at least 20 feet. Rat jumped back in genuine alarm as the plastic scenery above the drum riser began to melt and crumple. He recalled the fire department's emergency plan: 'But could I remember the code word? Could I ****!'

In a blind panic, Rat realised the only way to try and stop the fire was to kick the drums over. Smash them up, in fact. So the studio audience, production team and viewing public were treated to possibly the most outrageous example of gratuitous equipment destruction ever as Rat manically kicked the flaming drums around the stage.

The sound team, also panicking, created some wailing guitar feedback to hide the fact that the soundtrack was not in synch with what was happening on camera. This made the whole spectacle seem even more outrageous to the unsuspecting viewer. So the producer got what she wanted after all, and a little bit extra...

It just goes to show that, even when a band is miming on

TV, you can always rely on the drummer to go the extra mile to achieve maximum dramatic effect.

'Super!'

BATTLE OF THE BANDS

In 1978 punk was at its height. I was drumming with Sid Sideboard And The Chairs —not really punk but fast R&B with a punky edge. On one occasion we were on the motorway going to a gig when suddenly we were overtaken by a coach load of people on their way to a Ruts show.

The Ruts were huge on the punk scene and out of our league, but the strange thing was their fans were leaning out of the windows trying to catch our attention. Then we noticed that they were all wearing Sid Sideboard badges. We were chuffed. We figured they must have been at one of our gigs because we gave out free badges instead of tickets.

Thirty-one years later I finally got to meet Dave Ruffy, drummer with The Ruts. Since those days he has notched up a hugely impressive CV, including playing with Aztec Camera, The Waterboys, Sinead O'Connor, Alison Moyet and more recently Marc Almond. I met him in his local pub in South London, where he told me this story from those punk days.

It's 1979 and The Ruts are on stage at the West Runton Pavilion, playing a high energy set to a highly excited punk audience. All the usual ingredients of a good punk gig are in place, including the spasmodic exchange of gob and spit between guitarists and audience. Then suddenly, from behind my kit, I see Captain Sensible and Rat Scabies from The

Damned walking nonchalantly across the front of the stage eating fish and chips from newspaper wrapper. They completely ignore the proceedings, as if they are taking a pleasant afternoon stroll through the park.

I realise that this is just another wind up, par for the course when one punk band supports another, and on this particular UK tour The Ruts are supporting The Damned. The previous night the Captain (guitarist and sometime bass player with The Damned) sat reading the paper at the back of the audience throughout our entire set. After the gig, myself and the rest of the band decide it's time to get The Damned back, so a plan is hatched.

There is one song in The Damned's set in which Rat sings lead vocals – his self-penned song entitled 'Burglar'. Usually I do the band a favour and sit in on drums for this song. It's decided that I will wear a vicious-looking thug/burglar's mask while playing, thus taking the piss out of Rat's song behind his back. OK, it might get a little hot and uncomfortable but so what? It's only for one song.

We plan this little prank for the third-last night of the tour. Rat has been giving us advice on the do's and don'ts of touring, and one pearl of wisdom is that you should never do a big wind up on the last night because your victims will be expecting it. Do it on the penultimate night instead. So, as The Damned are therefore likely to be expecting a wind up on the second-last night, The Ruts plan it for the night before that.

So it transpires that on the said day we are travelling to Leicester. The journey takes us through some beautiful, rural countryside. As I stare out of the van window at the expanse of potato fields, someone spies a small farm up ahead, just off the main road. On the roadside is a sign, which says: 'Manure for sale'.

This sparks another idea. Why not walk on stage during Rat's burglar song, dressed as a burglar and carrying a swag bag, or rather, a bin liner full of manure? And then dump it on the front of the stage?

So the van pulls up outside the farm and Dave, Malcolm, Segs and Paul approach the farm entrance. There is a little bearded man with a broad country accent at a shop counter.

'And what can I do for you gentlemen?'

'We'd like to buy some manure please.'

'What type of manure?'

'Err... what types have you got?'

'Horse and cow excrement, chicken and hen faeces...'

'Actually it doesn't really matter – we only want it to for a joke.'

'A joke?'

'Well, a prank really.'

'Ahh! You want to play a prank on someone! I've got just the thing for you...'

'Really?'

'Yeah, you don't want any of this shit!'

'No?'

'I've got some much better stuff out the back...'

'What's that?'

'Pig shit.'

So it is that we resume our journey, complete with a huge bin liner full of pig manure on board. It's decided that when The Ruts' set finishes, I must pretend to be ill so that the Captain will have to play drums on 'Burglar' as he's a half-decent drummer and knows the song. That way I can walk on stage as the burglar with the swag bag full of pig's manure, accompanied by my three band mates.

Finally the van pulls up at Leicester University and we're directed to the De Montfort Hall, a grand and pristine building on the outside and beautifully decorated on the inside, with great oak doors and wood-panelled walls all round the interior of the hall. As the roadies set up the PA and back line, Malcolm and myself hide the bin liner and mask behind the stage.

The bands sound check and then the doors open at 7.30pm. Hundreds of students pour in, plus a healthy contingent of Damned and Ruts fans. The crowd is very boisterous and the gig goes well. Then The Damned take the stage. Helped by Malcolm, Paul and Segs, I drag the black sack to the side of the stage.

Towards the end of their set, it's time for Rat Scabies to sing 'Burglar'. He leaves his drums and takes up position at the front of the stage. The Captain takes over on drums. The song begins. I put the burglar mask on. Then, accompanied by my band mates, I walk on stage and empty the entire contents of the black bag on the front of the stage, in between Rat and bass player Algy Ward. The look in their eyes tells me that I had better leave quickly, so I saunter off to the side of the stage. However, Malcolm, Segs and Paul decide to hang around. Rat and Algy do not look at all pleased, although the Captain is pissing himself at the back, as is singer Dave Vanian.

Then it all kicks off. Rat throws some at Segs, who throws

some back at Rat. Algy throws some at Malcolm, who returns the gesture. Then Paul Fox makes a big mistake. He throws some into the crowd, who presumably think the whole thing is a planned punk bonanza and are more than happy to join in. Not only that, the stuff smells so bad that it actually makes everyone quite cross.

For my own safety I remain off stage, watching what is possibly the ultimate statement in a culture that takes delight in celebrating the mutual exchange of natural bodily waste. As more and more excrement flies between stage and audience, the battle spreads around the front of the hall. Then Segs gets pushed off stage into the crowd. 'Kill himmmm!' Dave Vanian shouts through the mic in a long, low drawl.

He's only joking, but the crowd respond to his suggestion with enthusiasm. I watch as Paul and Malcolm eventually manage to pull Segs out of the crowd. At this point, I decide it might be time to leave, so I leg it back to the hotel. I take a quick shower (although I'm probably the only one who isn't covered in shit), then Malcolm and Paul arrive. A while later, Segs arrives without his shirt and smelling worse than anything they have ever smelled before. He'd got lost and had to hitch a lift back. (I notice that somehow he's found time to draw a shirt and collar round his neck in felt pen.)

Then the tour manager arrives back at the hotel. The news is not good. Apparently the roadies are refusing to pack away the gear and Asktam, the PA company, are threatening to go home. So if we don't want the last two nights to be cancelled, we all have to go back and clear it up ourselves, including our chums in The Damned.

When we arrive back at the hall, what meets our eyes is almost unbelievable. A vile steam is rising from the floor filling the hall, enveloping all and sundry, including those lovely panelled walls. The heat from the lights has combined with the combination of sweat, gob and pig manure to create a festering mass which smells almost unbearable. We all bow our heads in shame as both bands receive an almighty bollocking from Asktam. Then we set about wiping leads, speakers, mixing desks, drums, cymbals and everything else which the assembled crew refuse to touch.

To make things worse, during the final two performances of the tour, a vile smell seeps out from the fold-back monitor speakers onto the stage while we are playing. You can't cover a PA system in excrement and expect to clean it all out in a day. Still, never mind. The last gigs are a roaring success and everyone gets paid.

I arrive home having completed a successful support tour with one of the UK's most outrageous punk bands and having executed the most effective punk wind up of all time. In fact, you could say I'm as happy as a pig in shit.

Whenever there's a wind up or practical joke to be played, you can guarantee that the drummer will be selected as the individual best suited to carry it out. It's as if we are programmed for mischief simply because we have chosen to play the drums.

A Bunch Of Lightweights

Rick Buckler was drummer with new wave icons The Jam from their formation in 1977 until Paul Weller left the band in 1982. Rick worked closely with bass player Bruce Foxton to create a particularly distinctive rhythm section that would form an integral part of the sound behind Paul Weller's songs.

Following The Jam's split, Rick joined Time UK. Recently he has toured with Bruce Foxton in a band called From The Jam, but left that band in September 2009. Rick told me about a little band rivalry in the good old days.

In 1976 punk had been around for a couple of years, but none of the big names had been signed to a record label. So there was a small amount of speculation among the punk bands as to who would get signed first and release their first single. This set the scene for some friendly rivalry. As it happened, The Damned got there first with the release of their first single 'New Rose'.

Soon after that The Jam were in the offices of Polydor, having secured our own record deal. Someone warned us that The Damned were sending us a 'surprise' copy of their first album. The Damned had a reputation for being a bit leery, and as we did not know what to expect, I thought that we should get in first and send them a little something. So I took a copy of our first album into the toilet and filled it.

I carefully wrapped it up for the post (first class, of course) and put it in the out tray of the A&R department office. It sat there for a few days before being sent.

As predicted, a parcel turned up for us from The Damned. Understandably, nobody at Polydor wanted to open it. So, with some trepidation, we cautiously peeled it apart, expecting something indescribably nasty. We needn't have worried. They had sent us a copy of their album, smeared with jam.

Of course, not all outrageous behaviour is attributed to the punk era. Neither is some behaviour described necessarily as outrageous. Drummers can often be accused of simply being mildly rude, sometimes even with the best intentions...

BREAKING THE ICE

Dylan Howe is not only the drummer with The Blockheads (since 1998), he is also an accomplished bandleader, session musician and composer. His father is Yes guitarist Steve Howe, with whom he has worked on several projects over the years, including the Steve Howe Trio with Hammond organist Ross Stanley. The band toured the UK and Canada in 2007/2008 and in March 2010 to promote their live album *Travelling*.

With the exception of a few hints from Yes drummer Bill Bruford, plus some brief sessions with Bob Armstrong and Jonathan Mover, Dylan is essentially self-taught. As well as working with top producers like Trevor Horn, John Leckie and Nigel Godrich, Dylan's session and live work includes Paul McCartney, Ray Davies, Mick Jones, Damon Albarn, Nick Cave and Gabrielle. He also recently joined Wilko Johnson's trio and has led his own jazz groups since 2002, with five albums as leader to his name. He cites his main influences as Roy Haynes, Elvin Jones, Tony Williams, Philly-Jo Jones, Al Jackson Jr, Dennis Davis, Steve Gadd and Bernard Purdie.

So, what with that and The Blockheads, you could say

Dylan's got his work cut out. He told me about something cringingly embarrassing that happened when he was called up to do a one-off gig in London's Soho.

When you're a freelance musician, you are often thrown together with complete strangers in new situations, so it's always nice to find a way to relax around each other as quickly as possible. It can be a bit awkward at first, so you're hoping you can find something to talk about. It's not always that easy, though, especially when the odds are stacked against you. One such occasion springs to mind. It was about 15 years ago, but I can still remember it as if I'm there right now...

I receive a call asking me to do a last-minute gig at the Pizza Express on Dean Street with the singer Gill Manly. It's obviously a pick-up group that have never rehearsed or played together before so I arrive early, keen and a little bit nervous.

After a quick soundcheck and mini-rehearsal, it's time for the inevitable pre-gig break and free meal, during which everyone has to sit at a table together and make somewhat stilted conversation. As drummers and bass players usually have a kind of affinity under these circumstances, I opt to sit on a separate table with the bass player, who happens to be an older and more experienced musician, complete with beard and corduroys. In fact, I feel much like a beginner as I try to strike up conversation.

'So, is this a regular gig for you?'

'Grunt.'

'It's my first time here. I quite like these one-off gigs though...'

'Grunt.'

'Err, Gill seems quite nice. You know, easy to work with...'

'Grunt.'

'I think I'll go for an American hot...' I spend the next 10 minutes looking around the room in an attempt to escape from the incommunicative void to which I have been consigned. When my pizza comes, I wolf it down at an unfathomably swift rate and decide that my exit strategy should be to have a cigarette. This was in the days when smoking was not regarded as pure evil. I light a cigarette and, not wanting to be rude, move my chair slightly away from my new rhythm section comrade.

Upon lighting my cigarette, my dinner date gives me an indignant look and shifts further away on the table. I feel even more awkward. Then we actually have a conversation: 'Sorry, does this bother you?'

'Well, yes it does a bit. Maybe you could put it out?'

'Fair enough, I'll put it out.' I flick some ash into the ashtray before taking one last drag. Unfortunately, at this point the air conditioning above our heads decides to fire itself up, propelling the entire contents of the ashtray onto his newly presented and mint-looking side salad, over which his fork is poised. I look in dismay as the once green leaves now feature not only the popular Pizza Express dressing but also a generous sprinkling of dark grey fag ash.

He gives me a look, rather like that of an exasperated teacher about to scold a foolish and unruly child. Or like Oliver Hardy might look at Stan Laurel under similar circumstances. In a state of panic I try to blow the ash off.

This sends the rest of the ash onto the remains of his pizza.

I get the feeling he is about to explode when it is announced that we must take the stage area for tonight's performance. Saved by the bell. We then embark on a speechless but sadly memorable gig – four people playing on their own on the same stage. Ouch.

SECTION 5

NAUGHTY!

Drummers, Tch… Tch…

Sometimes, when a band has just started a song at a live gig, the guitarist or bass player will turn to tell the drummer to slow down. Not as a way of instigating a dramatic, premature ending to the song, but rather they are suggesting that the song is being played too fast.

Well, OK. It's the drummer's job to regulate the tempo and speed during songs. So if you need something regulated, he's the man to see about it. The problem is, the drummer feels accused, as if the implication is that it's his fault in the first place. Usually, however, the song will have been started with a guitar or keyboard intro. So not only is the drummer feeling that he's been accused of getting the speed wrong in the first place, he is now being asked to make an even bigger fool of himself by deliberately slowing down.

The drummer now has two choices. He can deliberately slow the tempo down to the taste of whoever has requested it, which will sound awful and the audience will probably notice and think he's being sluggish and playing badly. Alternatively, he can flatly refuse to slow down, which will give him a reputation for being a stubborn and unhelpful player.

The point is, a drummer is generally supposed to keep time, not change it. So if he suddenly messes with the established speed, be it right or wrong, it will sound awful. And he will get the blame...

DON'T MESS WITH THE BOSS

Paul Murphy is a highly experienced session drummer, who has played with Fatima Mansions, Dannii Minogue, Rhatigan, Guy Chadwick, Superior and many top West End shows. This story takes us back to 1996 when Paul was playing in a band backing PJ Proby in Bill Kenwright's *Elvis: The Musical* in London's West End. The show went through the various stages of Elvis' life and featured three people playing Elvis; young, middle and old (Vegas).

Like all drummers who play stage shows, Paul knows that many classic crooners tend to sing behind the beat in order to create greater dramatic effect, especially during love ballads. Lines often appear to end later than expected, sometimes lingering precariously on into the next phrase of the song. The really good singers master the art with considerable expertise. Of course, it's important for the rest of the band to ignore this deviation in order for it to work properly. The drummer needs to be acutely aware of the song's natural timing, sticking to a fairly rigid structure so the singer has the freedom to move the lines around, confident in the knowledge that everything else will be played exactly as expected.

I am seated behind my kit on my drum rostrum on stage at

the opening night. It's the Prince Of Wales Theatre in Leicester Square and the house is packed. The show is going well and we're well into the second half. The time has come to feature the third incarnation of Elvis Presley as an older star performing in Vegas, played by PJ Proby. I'm feeling confident about the rest of the show because rehearsals with PJ have been going very well. Although he sings very far behind the beat – sometimes a whole chord change behind the rest of the band – I've got the measure of his style and know how to take these variations on board. So I'm a bit surprised when, after a couple of numbers, he turns and gives me a dirty look. I am inclined to put that down to first-night nerves, or maybe I misread the expression on his face – perhaps he was smirking in fun?

But then he does it again. And again! Eventually he articulates himself more clearly and indicates that the song is too fast and he wants me to slow things down. So I do my best to reduce the pace as subtly as possible, which is much more difficult than speeding up gradually. The real worry is, if it all goes embarrassingly wrong, it will be my fault. I will be ultimately responsible for whatever transpires as the result of a random request made by the singer.

The next night I am playing the same song, this time paying careful attention to the tempo. I'm pleased because the speed seems just right and the band is in a nice, tight groove. But then it happens again. PJ turns round and gives me another filthy look. I'm wondering what can be the matter when he indicates that the song is too *slow* this time. So I oblige by speeding up a little. I notice as the gig goes on that PJ is becoming continually more agitated.

The same behaviour continues throughout every show until, one night, I am sitting with the rest of the band in the bar opposite the theatre, enjoying an after-show drink, when the musical director (the man who originally booked the band) approaches. He is smiling in an amused kind of way as he says: 'You had better get a lawyer!'

'W-why?'

'PJ says you'd better hire a good lawyer because he is going to sue you for deliberately changing the tempos of the songs in the show.'

'That's not true. Why would I want to change the speeds of the songs?'

'Deliberately to annoy him, apparently. He says you speed up or slow down at random. Just to piss him off. And he's just about had enough!'

'He can't be serious!'

'Don't worry! There's no need to take it seriously – there's nothing wrong with your playing as far as I can see. PJ's just looking for something else to complain about.'

Although I am relieved that the MD obviously hasn't taken PJ's accusations seriously, part of me thinks later as I'm on my way home: 'What if he's right? What if I am speeding up and slowing down but don't realise?' As a drummer that's about as bad as it gets! It could be the end of my career! And what if he did carry out his threat? Imagine the headline: DRUMMER IN COURT FOR SHIT TIME-KEEPING.'

As it happened, Proby never mentioned it again and a few shows later he left the show because he was becoming a nightmare to work with. Of course, there had been nothing wrong with Paul's time keeping, although he did get some good-natured ribbing about it during the rest of the run. It was just a case of good old-fashioned playground bullying. In fact, you can almost imagine PJ Proby and Paul Murphy as school children in a playground, PJ periodically kicking Paul's arse while the rest of the infant band look on.

Playing as a backing band for a singer is a bit like living under a kind of musical dictatorship. Whatever the guy says goes. If he thinks it's too fast or too slow, you can't argue. Sometimes he might be right, but that still does not necessarily mean it's appropriate to change the speed during the song, unless it is so hideously out that a change is unavoidable. But that never happens. As drummers, we are at the mercy of whatever whims happen to invade the mind of whoever is in charge, those whims often being a distorted perception of what is actually happening. But make no mistake, whatever appears to be wrong will be our fault. Moreover, anything else that sounds not quite right as a result of our attempts to rectify the situation will also end up being our fault...

As ever, if anyone is going to be the butt boy, you can bet your bottom dollar it'll be the drummer. As a drummer, being in control of the speed does invest you with a certain amount of power. This should rarely be abused, but there are sometimes occasions on which a little tinkering is irresistible and even justified...

MAD, BAD AND DANGEROUS

A DRUMMER'S REVENGE
ANOTHER TALE FROM NIGEL GLOCKNER OF SAXON

It's 1996 and Saxon are on tour in Sweden. The last encore of the night's proceedings is a medley of some of the more manic Saxon songs – 'Heavy Metal Thunder', 'Taking Your Chances', 'Stand Up and be Counted', 'Warrior' and 'Battlecry'.

After one show I am particularly tired so, after a couple of beers, I retire to my pit (bunk) on the tour bus. But some of the other guys, including some of the crew, happen to be in party mode and keep me awake most of the night. Of course, the next day they are all nursing terrible hangovers. And the next show is that night after a day's travelling. I figure it's time for my revenge.

The show goes well that night. By the time we get to the encore medley, the other guys are suffering but they've managed to deliver so far. However, the intro to the medley is a bit slow, so I decide it's time to speed things up a little. There are lot of double-kick triplets in these songs, which the guitarists have to latch onto, so at each waypoint I slowly notch up the tempo – hardly noticeable to a punter, who would just think the song is getting more intense.

As I keep doing this, a little more each time, it gets harder for the other guys to keep up. Halfway through they are really struggling. Their wrists are in agony and they have pained expressions on their faces.

We had a good laugh about it later. But the lesson was learned: That'll teach you to keep me awake!

As Nigel says, the punter would simply have seen the

grimaces as the ultimate expression of passionate frenzy –
little knowing that these rock gods were actually whimpering
at the sheer pain of it all. Apparently, according to the
guitarists, Nigel had a demonic grin on his face throughout
the whole incident!

But as well as time keeping and other musical issues,
drummers also tend to get the blame for all kinds of things
that go wrong in the travels of a working band...

TAKING THE BLAME

Tim Goldsmith is a highly accomplished session drummer
whose CV includes Alison Moyet, Tanita Tikaram,
Bananarama, Go West and Joan Armatrading. Tim had an
interesting experience back in 1992, on tour with a famous
black acoustic singer from the Midlands. The night in
question was a 3000-seater venue in Milton Keynes. The
other members of the singer's backing band were feeling a bit
jaded and hung over. In fact, some had enjoyed a quick hair
of the dog before the show...

The support act has finished and I am in the wings waiting to
go on. It's always a tense, nervous point in the proceedings. I
know when I get out there and start playing the buzz will be
as good as ever. I'm vaguely aware that the rest of the band are
a bit hung over and the worse for wear but I know that, as
professionals, the band is bound to deliver. The moment
arrives and I walk on stage as enthusiastic applause wells up
from the auditorium.

After the first few numbers I get the feeling that things are
beginning to drag a bit musically, but the crowd don't seem to

notice and, after all, they don't know the guys aren't feeling 100 per cent. So I carry on in the hope that things will get into a tighter groove as the gig progresses. Eventually, the female singer/songwriter and leader of the band (my boss) makes an announcement to the audience: 'Excuse me everyone, I'm just going to have a word with the drummer.'

She then turns from the mike, walks up to the drum riser and says: 'Tim, can I have a word?' I bend down and offer my ear as she speaks: 'It's all a bit sluggish tonight. Can you kind of beef it up a bit?'

I nod in the affirmative as she walks back to the mic and says to the audience: 'Sorry about that, I just had to have a word with the drummer.'

I wince a little inwardly. But then she goes on to say: 'In fact, is there another drummer in the house?'

I am stunned into embarrassment that soon gives way to inner fury. Although the comment is meant as a kind of joke, it is neither funny nor appropriate – and is wholly at my expense. Of course, I have no option but to try and laugh along awkwardly with the joke and carry on.

Alternatively, Tim could have gone for a curry. He have could treated the joke with the utter contempt it deserves. He could have put down his sticks and left the building via the backstage exit, hailed a cab and found the nearest Indian restaurant. Sod the lot of them; singer, band and capacity crowd.

Of course, Tim did the sensible thing and carried on. But he did play the next song with astonishing vigour, attacking the kit with all the might and subtle anger of a drummer who

Above: Adam Ficek
from Babyshambles.

© *Steve Cook*
seekerphoto.co.uk

Below: Albert Buchard,
founder member of
Blue Öyster Cult.

© *Carol DeCarlo*

Indie rock drummer Andy Burrows.

Above left: Andy Theakstone plays with Get Cape. Wear Cape. Fly.
© Tom Canty

Above right: Girlschool drummer Denise Dufort. © Courtesy of Denise Dufort

Below left: From The Ruts to Marc Almond, Dave Ruffy's career has included Aztec Camera and The Waterboys, among others.

Below right: Slade's original drummer Don Powell continues with the group today.
© Lise Lyng Falkenberg

Above: Friend of Keith Moon and Argent drummer Bob Henrit.

Below: Brett 'Buddy' Ascott on stage with '70s punk legends.

Above: Blockheads drummer, band leader and son of Yes guitarist Steve Howe – Dylan. © *Jerry Tremaine*

Below: Everett Morton, drummer with The Beat. © *Yad Jaura*

Above: Among his many gigs John Lingwood has played for Manfred Mann's Earth Band.
© Helen Hardy

Below: Steve Phyphers plays with '60s covers band The Overtures. *© Joe Alvarez*

Above: Former Libertine and now Dirty Pretty Thing musician Gary Powell. © *Tim Wenzlick*

Below: Hugely experienced Marillion drummer Ian Mosley. © *Joe Del Tufo*

The Damned's Rat Scabies.

© Denis O'Regan

has been very badly treated. But imagine if he had actually walked out and gone for a curry: you're just finishing your meal when your mobile rings. It's your famous singer boss:

'Tim! Where the hell are you?'

'I was a bit peckish so I went for a curry. How are things at your end?'

'What do you mean, how are things at my end! I've had to stop the set and call an early interval!'

'So there wasn't another drummer in the house then?'

'It was only a joke! I'm sorry – please come back and finish the gig?'

'On one condition.'

'What's that?'

'You pay for my curry...'

If a band isn't playing quite up to scratch, either through a lack of collective energy or because some people are hung over, the drummer will always get the blame. Even if he stayed sober the night before, as Tim had done. It's as though there's an established code of practice which allows drummers to become the scapegoat for anything that goes wrong.

In Tim's case, the gig actually finished very well and he continued on what was to be a very successful tour. Eventually the whole episode became water under the professional bridge and Tim did get a belated apology from the famous singer. But no curry.

Do You Really Want To Hurt Me?

Jon Moss was the drummer with '80s icons Culture Club, playing on all their records and touring extensively all over the world. Before that he had played with a number of bands including Adam And The Ants, London and The Damned. He currently plays with two bands, DanMingo and Dirth.

I met Jon in his favourite café in Hampstead, which he had kindly arranged to be open just for our meeting. He told me about a Culture Club incident back in the early '80s when Culture Club were at the height of their success…

The band are on tour in the US and tonight they are playing at an enormous old theatre somewhere in the Midwest. The boys arrive at the venue just before show time and are escorted back stage to their dressing rooms to prepare and get made up. When they are ready to go on, security point them in the direction of an arrow sign which says 'Stage'. George and Jon lead the way while the rest of the band follow. They walk down a long corridor, which leads them to a kind of T-junction. An arrow points to the right, so they duly take a right. This corridor leads to some steps and then veers left. Jon remarks that it seems to be taking forever as they come to another right turn. As the band round the corner they are met with the sight of a large guy in overalls sitting on a bench next to some metal piping, holding a spanner.

'Err, excuse me, is this the way to the stage?' Jon asks.

'No way man, wrong place!' He taps the pipe to his left as if reprimanding them for their folly.

'Well, where do we go?'

The man points at George: 'Hey! You that Boy George!!!'

'Yes and we really need to get…'

'KummaKummaKummaKummaKumma kumeeleonn!'

'Yes, that's the one but please tell us where the stage…'

'That my daughter's favourite song!'

'Ah, that's nice…'

'That and "Doo Yooo Reely Wanta Hurrrt Meeee"!'

Jon butts in: 'There are lots of people like your daughter waiting for George to sing those songs right now in the theatre, so pleeease can you tell us the way?'

'Ahh of course! Go back the way you came and make a left at the end, then sharp right up the steps and that's the stage door!'

The band scurry back down the corridors. They take the directions as instructed but find themselves in a props department, which is actually right underneath the stage. They realise they are completely lost. This is made worse by the fact they are about to be announced. George and Jon decide it's best for the others to go off in different directions to find the stage door and then return to tell them where it is. That way there would be more chance of success, rather than everyone getting lost together.

After the others have gone, an argument starts. 'You took the wrong turn back there…'

'No I didn't, it was you!'

'What do you mean? You were in front!'

'Yeah but you told me to go that way!'

Maybe it's pre-gig nerves combined with the panic of being lost, but a fight ensues. George pushes Jon, who pushes George back, but rather too hard as George reels backwards and falls into two mannequins, which in turn fall backwards into a props table. George lunges at Jon who is too quick for him and trips him sideways into a freestanding wardrobe, which then collapses on top of him.

Jon begins to laugh at the sight of Boy George lying flat out on the floor covered in mannequins, wigs and fancy scarves. After all, it's his natural habitat. Eventually the band make it to the stage, somewhat dishevelled and breathless. George runs up to his mic and gasps: 'Good evening, Philadelphia!'

They were in Texas...

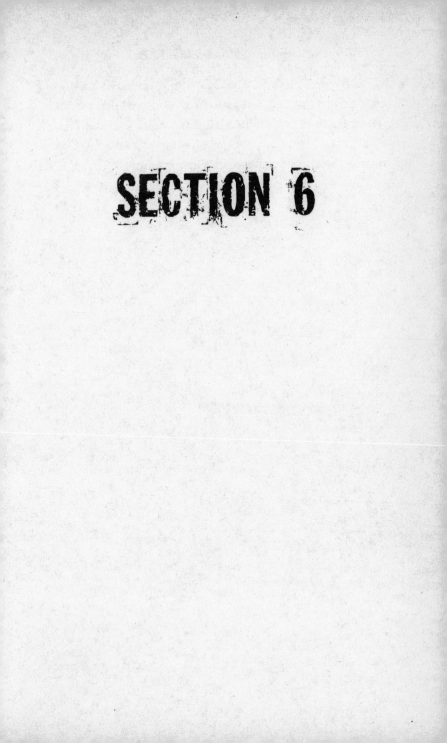

SECTION 6

UP TO MISCHIEF

Watch Out, There's A Drummer About...

If a member of the band is expected to behave like a child, it'll be the drummer. Maybe it's something to do with the nature of the instrument itself. After all, we are fully prepared to spend a lot of time at the outset bashing things really hard with bits of wood, until we learn the subtleties involved in playing to order. Even after that, the activity continues to involve a lot of banging. So when you're told to shut up, it can feel a bit like you've been told off for being naughty.

Sometimes, however, the level of castigation we are subjected to can be unexpectedly severe...

Extra-ordinary Behaviour

Here's another incident featuring top session player Tim Goldsmith. A famous Irish singer from a well known '70s/'80s group had put a band together to do a big showcase for the launch of a new album and single in the mid-'80s. Two shows were planned: one at The Greyhound in west

London and a live *Old Grey Whistle Test* performance which would also feature Dave Stewart from Eurythmics and Richard Branson, who had just signed him...

I'm at a rehearsal in the much-praised Nomis studios in Kensington. The band consists of sensational players: John Mackenzie on bass, David Rhodes from Peter Gabriel's band, Davey Payne (the wacky sax player from The Blockheads), Pete Thoms (he beret-wearing trombonist responsible for things like Thomas Dolby's 'Hyperactive', Pat Seymour on keys, three crack backing vocalists, and yours truly on tubs.

The band is sounding great as we punch out tracks like 'A Good Heart' from the new album. It's then decided to run through a version of 'When a Man Loves a Woman', a thoughtful delivery of a classic song. The band reaches a part of the song where the dynamics are lowered and the feel is soft and light for a few bars. I spy the bell of my brand-new 20-inch K Zildjian ride cymbal and, in a moment of inspiration, I feel it is the perfect opportunity to add to the texture of the sound by striking the bell on the first beat of the bar: a perfectly reasonable way to add a tasteful touch to a sensitive passage in the song. What happens next is totally unexpected.

I look over at our leader as he bends down, hugging the microphone in a kind of frenzied passion. He seems almost convulsed. He then leaps up into the air and turns to me with a demonic look of a man possessed by fury. In an instant he has transformed from the sensitive singer of an old love song to a murderous madman. Purple with rage, he screams at me like a wailing hyena from Londonderry.

'How fucking dare you! Don't you fucking dare do that in my song, you bastard! Don't ever do that again!'

My jaw drops in disbelief and I feel my heart pounding with uncontrollable embarrassment. The other band members look at me in horror and then, unable to endure my discomfort any longer, look down at the floor. There is total silence. I find myself choking back unwanted tears of shear mortification – the kind of indignant feeling I remember having as a child when unjustly scolded. Yet this is a man who has hired me as a professional, adult human being. I thought he was a grown up too.

But in the heady world of rock 'n' roll anything can happen, apparently.

Poor Tim. But also spare a thought for the singer. It happens all the time. Some nobody becomes a somebody, loses sight of reality and forgets how to behave. Sometimes this enters the realms of madness. How could the sound of a simple cymbal bell cause such a hysterical reaction? The fact is, the ego concerned honestly believes that they are right. Sir Elton John once famously rang the concierge of a hotel he was staying in. The problem? He was trying to write a song, but the wind outside was so noisy it was putting him off. Could the concierge control the weather, please? Even we normally down-to-earth drummers aren't immune. A certain Mr Moon was famous for behaviour which might have been considered a little out of the ordinary.

Tim's reaction to this outburst was to continue with the rehearsal, which was now somewhat subdued. Afterwards, the bass player congratulated him on keeping his cool. Of course, as in Tim's case, when you're 24 years old and hungry for top gigs, you tend to take stuff like that on the chin. However, as Tim reflected years later, had he been seven or eight years older, the singer in question might have had more than the sound of a cymbal bell to cope with on that occasion. 'Like a Pro-Mark 5A drumstick stuck in his head.'

Andy Wells, drummer with The Slaves and erstwhile drummer for Meat Loaf, recalls a time when he was reprimanded for almost everything he did.

I used to play with a blues guitar player who was a real purist, one of those guys who thought drummers are simply there to be tolerated, an irritation that gets in the way of the music. When we were out playing he would come out with stuff like, 'That bloody drummer, he couldn't shuffle if you tied his shoelaces together.' Or, 'See that drummer? He wouldn't swing if you hung him.'

I remember a particular conversation we had after one gig: 'Wellsy dear boy, what were you doing during my solo?'

'Oh, you know, just trying out a couple of new fills...'

'In future, please can you not do that, because it really does sound like you've decided to put up a shed.'

I once went on a short five-gig tour in Ireland with a band called Texas Flood. I was standing in for their regular drummer, who was busy touring with the Glen Millar tribute band. We went to Enniscorthy, Dublin, Kilkenny and Thomastown. As most people know, Ireland is famous for, among other things, its Guinness. And I like Guinness.

Occasionally, while the guitarists rehearsed their parts in their bedrooms a few hours before a gig, I would pop out to explore. Inevitably, I would end up in a local Irish pub with a Guinness. One, maybe two, but not five or seven. But I know it genuinely worried the guitarists. I could imagine the conversation:

'Oh no, he's off again.'

'Someone better go and check on him – make sure he doesn't have too much Guinness.'

Paul Murphy, the bass player, would come and check on me and we'd drink Guinness together. Well, he is Irish and likes it too. We used to joke that I should have been put on reins.

Of course, as a drummer you can get into trouble from a very early age...

SIX OF THE BEST

Albert Bouchard is a founder member of American rock band Blue Öyster Cult. Formed in 1967, the band's hard-edged approach to rock led them being widely recognised as pioneers of heavy metal. In 1981, Albert left the band to work on a solo album, although his record label put it out as a BÖC record – *Imaginos*. He later took a second break from the group, playing with a variety of artists including Helen Wheels, The Mamas And The Papas, Peter Noone and Spencer Davis. In 1994 he formed The Brain Surgeons and has since performed with his brother Joe on a disc by X-Brothers.

Albert kindly sent me this little story, which takes us back to when he was a mere toddler.

It's Albert's birthday. He is just three years old. As it's Memorial Day weekend in the USA, his folks have taken him to watch a parade of local servicemen in his hometown, Clayton NY. He is fascinated by the marching band as it passes, especially by the drummers with their loud drum rolls and cymbal crashes. For someone of such a young age, it is pure magic. Albert is hooked.

He is now on a mission to get a snare drum from his parents. Eventually they give in and buy him a drum. Not a snare, exactly, but a little tin drum with some tiny sticks. Albert is thrilled and when his folks can stand it, spends all his time banging away on his new drum.

Early one morning, as dawn is breaking, Albert's mum wakes slowly to the faint sound of Albert banging on his drum. At first she thinks she might be dreaming because it's not the usual loud rap that she is used to, but soft and distant. After a while, she decides to investigate.

Oh dear. There is no sign of Albert in his bedroom, only his discarded diaper on the floor. She panics. Then out of the bedroom window she spies Albert. He is marching proudly down the middle of the street, banging his drum with all the gusto of a marching bandsman. As she hurries downstairs and into the street she reflects, a little angrily, that it really is time he was potty-trained.

When Albert is finally caught and brought back indoors, he is the unwilling recipient of several rhythmic strokes to the backside, administered with a spiked hairbrush, and he is forbidden to touch a drum for many years to come.

Ahh, bless. Drummers have a habit of annoying people from a very early age, but it's interesting to reflect that, if a young musician is going to be subjected to a form of punishment traditionally associated with headmasters of public schools in the middle of the last century, it'll be a drummer.

This sense that as drummers we are naturally to be placed under certain authoritative jurisdiction seems to crop up on a fairly regular basis. Sometimes we simply have to jolly well do as we are told...

IN THE BACK, SPIKE!

Like most drummers, I was in a series of bands at school, doing gigs in my local area. Sometimes we would travel a little further afield, which would mean transport complications. We usually did our best with a couple of cars as we couldn't afford a van, but whenever these jaunts occurred, it always seemed to be me that drew the short straw when it came to personal comfort. I recall one such occasion back in 1976, when I was just 17.

We were on the road one night. That is, we were travelling in a Triumph Herald soft top on the M1. As you probably know, Triumph Heralds are not large vehicles. They are, in fact, very small, designed as lightweight run-arounds for singles or couples to indulge in everyday life – short trips to work, a day in the countryside with a couple of friends and perhaps a picnic in the boot. You can even take the top down on a hot summer's day, lean back comfortably and wave at passers by.

On this occasion, however, the soft-top Triumph Herald had been deployed for an entirely different purpose. We were making the return journey back to Watford after a gig at a student function somewhere in Oxford. Bass player in the driver's seat, guitarist next to him in the front passenger seat and me, the drummer, in the back. Plus all our equipment in the back as well. This consisted of drums (no cases in those days – we were only 17 and had no money), guitars, a Selmer amp and a couple of speakers. Oh, and some mike stands. The roof was securely on and every item had been crammed in after I had established myself in the back, so that every bit of space available could be put to good use. I seem to remember there was a guitar in the front, held between the guitarist's legs. However, the driver needed all his available space to manoeuvre the vehicle.

To start with, I looked at the situation philosophically. After all, it wasn't that far – about an hour – and someone had to travel in the back with the equipment. And although the various hard edges of drums and amplifiers were digging into my flesh with unrelenting persistence, I felt that, for the length of this journey at least, it was worth it for rock 'n' roll. After all, what was I? Some kind of wimp? Rolling with the bumps and grinds was all part of being on the road to success. That's the way I saw it.

Until night fell, that is.

About half way into our journey, around midnight, Warren, our bass player and driver, declared that he'd had enough of driving for the time being. He was beginning to nod off, which is not good on a motorway, and needed to get 20 minutes shut-eye in order to carry on. Justin, our guitarist, had not yet learned to drive so he couldn't take over, and I couldn't drive either. So the decision was made to pull over onto the hard shoulder for 20 minutes so Warren could 'power nap'. Having pulled over, the boys in the front of the car fidgeted and moved around until they found their optimum sleeping position. This had the effect of interfering with the already cramped conditions in the back of the car, presenting me with fresh bumps and grinding pressures to contend with. 'Ah well,' I thought, 'only 20 minutes and we'll be on our way again.' Not so.

After about five minutes the snoring started. In unison. And as the boys fell gradually more deeply asleep, the volume of the snoring increased accordingly. Try as I might, my discomfort was so intense that I could not enjoy anything like the same repose. In fact, as the sound of their peaceful abandon became louder and louder, it emphasised my predicament even more. I was unable to move to any significant degree, which was again reflected by the movements of the two in front as they shifted and turned in their seats in the customary style of those enjoying a good sound sleep.

After about an hour, my patience sapped, I tried to wake them up. I called to them politely (after all, they were tired, bless): 'Ahem... cough... cough... err, chaps... hello? Time's marching on?'

There was no response. In fact, the snoring seemed to get louder, as if my verbal gesticulations had occasioned some kind of renewed vigour – almost in defiance of any attempt to interrupt their sweet solace. To be fair, I didn't shout. It was more like an apologetic cry for help. Rather like Sgt Wilson in

Dad's Army. I even considered trying to escape, but this was a two-door car, not a four-door. I was trapped. I thought I might as well light a cigarette to help pass the time.

This was not easy as my matches were in my back pocket, which was difficult to access given the amount of wood and metal wedged around me. I managed it eventually and lit a cigarette, but this actually made matters worse, partly because the sound of snoring was now compounded by the sounds of snorting and coughing caused by the smoke. After a very short time I was desperate to put the fag out, but the windows were closed and there was no way I could reach the handles. And, of course, there were none in the back.

So now I was stuck in the back of a car full of smoke with what sounded like a couple of wheezing old men in the front. Eventually I managed to dispose of the cigarette through a slight rip in the canvas of the soft top that I discovered adjacent to my right ear.

As time passed, the sound of motorway traffic began to die away and, as the night took hold, the snoring from the front resided into a gentle breathing – an indication to me that my companions had reached that blissful repose commonly associated with deep, dreamless sleep. My neck was beginning to ache as I tried to move, inch by inch, from one head position to another. I remember slipping periodically into some kind of momentary delirium, only to be swiftly awoken by the adverse sleeping conditions which I had come to accept with a kind of resigned and vaguely amused madness: a symptom of sleep deprivation. I remember thinking this is how they used to torture people in Japan.

Eventually, of course, the birds began to stir from their

own sweet slumber and started singing again in the distant trees. This was accompanied by the sound of distant vehicles approaching. First one would pass. Then another, a minute or so later, followed by a couple more not far behind; until the motorway began to come alive again. All this sounded particularly wonderful to me, as it signified the breaking of day and the light at the end of this particular tunnel.

Now to the boys in front. They began to wake up but, not being in any particular hurry, this was a slow and laborious process. Laborious for me, that is. For their part, they behaved as though they were waking from a long and refreshing repose that was sure to guarantee all the feisty energies needed to negotiate the dawning of a new day. This manifested itself in much luxurious yawning, fidgeting and lengthy stretching of arms and legs – which served only to restructure the positioning of certain items in the back, once again presenting me with fresh challenges with regard to pressure points on my legs and torso.

And eventually: 'You alright in the back there, Spike?'

There was no real answer to this question. Not one that would have done me any favours. So I adopted the Sgt Wilson approach once more.

'Err, not at all bad considering. Do you think we could get going again... soon, perhaps?'

There seems to be an assumption that drummers are more adaptable to uncomfortable or even dangerous circumstances than other musicians. If someone has to travel in the back of the van among precariously stacked speakers, drums and musical equipment, why is it that the drummer seems the obvious choice? So often during the days when I was in 'bands with vans' did I find myself holding onto large metal boxes and containers, attempting to wedge objects against the back wall of a box Luton which was bumping and sliding around at some ridiculous speed either on a motorway or down a dodgy dirt track. Occasionally, the music coming from the radio in the front of the van would stop and I would hear a muffled voice: 'You alright in the back there Spike?'

The tone of voice always embodied a kind of resigned sympathy. It was as though, for some reason, behaving like Buster Keaton kind of goes with the job of being a drummer.

RIGHT FIRST TIME

Studio work has its ups and downs for all musicians and most will agree that to deliver reliably and consistently requires a certain discipline that can only be learned over time. Drummers, in particular, need to harness a special kind of mind set, simply because it's the only ingredient in the recording of a pop song that has to be right all the way through on any usable take. Although these days you can make adjustments to a drum track, it's still the one instrument on a band recording that generally needs to be right all the way through; drop-ins and overdubs are not usually an option. If there are any bits that the drummer might not be entirely happy with, he/she will have to live with them if they occur on a take that is chosen because the rest of the band's performance is considered to be so good that it's worth it.

Consequently, when a drummer miraculously delivers a spot-on performance on take one, it's something of a result for all concerned. The rest of the band can do any patching up that's needed and you can all move on to the next track, or whatever part of the proceedings is next on the schedule.

Tim Goldsmith remembers doing a session for the singer Vicki Brown (sadly now no longer with us) and the producer was her daughter, Sam Brown. The song was called 'Goldilocks' and the studio was Wisseloord in Holland.

After the usual couple of hours or so of getting the right drum sound and generally getting comfortable, everyone is in position and ready to go. We've had a couple of run-throughs and I'm confident that the backing track should be put to bed in three or four takes. Sam Brown, who's producing, is sitting comfortably in the control room with the engineer and gives a thumbs up as I hear through my cans (headphones), 'OK, let's go for a take.'

The take goes extraordinarily well drum wise. All the ingredients are there. The groove is set up nicely from the start, the accents are all crisp and the fills tastefully executed. And the overall feel is spot on all the way through. I hadn't expected to deliver my best performance on the first take, but I know instinctively that this really is the best way I am ever going to play that track. It is, in my opinion, the perfect take. And I should know, because I am the drummer after all.

So I and the rest of the musicians retire to the control room for the customary listen-back to the track. Everyone, including Sam, agrees that the drum track is, indeed, rather good. Very good, in fact. Spot on. Well done! However, there is some doubt as to whether the other guys were on top form on that take. Still, I reason that they can keep the drum track and the rest of the band can go again for take two. Job done, so to speak. But for some reason, it is unanimously decided that the whole band should all go for another take, drummer included.

But I know I'll never get it as good as that again, I remonstrate. It's not laziness, it's a fact. I can tell you as a professional player that you should keep that drum track. Sam and the engineer both disagree and reply jokingly: 'Well, you'll just have to go in there and knock another one out then, won't you?'

Under these circumstances, there is no way I can flatly refuse to 'knock another one out'. I would be accused of being a prima donna among other things. And Sam is the boss at the session at the end of the day. So, rather like a schoolchild who's been told he's going to have to jolly well pull his socks up, I go back in for a few more takes. Of course, the drumming on the final take is nowhere near as good in my opinion. In fact, *none* of the takes are anything like as good, but the 'perfect take' is consigned to history.

It's another example of what can sometimes happen when it comes to the drummer's perceived status in the general scheme of things. It's as though the nature of the instrument means that certain privileges with regard to overall decision-making are denied to you as a matter of course – in a kind of vaguely amused way. Rather like the way a teenager's radical opinions on world matters may be indulged for a while but ultimately dismissed when it's time for the grown-ups to get into serious debate.

In fact, some studio engineers are prone to speaking to drummers as if they are children. You turn up at the beginning of a session and deposit your drums in the corner of the playing area. The engineer comes in and looks at you almost mischievously, as if you've just plonked down your favourite set of tin soldiers and says cheekily: 'Don't worry, we'll have you sorted out in no time!' And another thing: why is it that some really clever technicians always talk to you in a silly voice?

Drummer: 'Could we possibly get a little delay on the snare? Especially in the quiet bit?'

Clever engineer: 'Aaawwwwww... tch... tch... eyeeee think we can just about manage that, Batman!'

COLD SHOT

Sometimes things can go inexplicably badly and it's glaringly obvious that the drummer is doing something horribly wrong. I once played a number so irredeemably wrongly that to this day I'm not quite sure how I did it. It was so catastrophically embarrassing that it deserves a mention.

It was when I first started playing with my old friends Texas Flood, a Stevie Ray Vaughan-based blues/rock band. It was probably my first gig with them at a place called George's Wine Bar in Bricket Wood, near St Albans in Hertfordshire. There had been no rehearsal but I managed to get the feel right and take my cues from Murph, the bass player, without any noticeable gaffes. The place was quite packed and the band had mentioned that I was new and unrehearsed, which seemed to be going down quite well. I felt good because I was winging it and everyone knew it. In short, it all gelled really nicely. Then came 'Cold Shot'.

This is a slow blues shuffle in 'swampy' style. You're

supposed to play it as though you are wading through a swamp, lazy and slightly behind the beat. What I did could not have been further away on the musical spectrum. I'd never heard the song before and asked Jeff the guitarist to play a bit before we started. He played the guitar rhythm part, which I completely misinterpreted as a staccato riff in 5/4 time. So instead of a nice, sleek blues feel, the band and audience were subjected to a Germanic rant in 5/4.

Now, you have to remember that this audience consisted mainly of people who had come specifically to hear blues/shuffle music you can dance to. Many were Stevie Ray Vaughan fans. Some actually tried to dance to this and ended up doing a strange combination of writhing and jerky movements that defied even the simplest of conventions with regard to basic dancing moves. By the desperation on Murph's face and the looks of complete disbelief that came my way from the others, it was clear that my misinterpretation of the basic rhythm was of such monstrous proportions that I was actually causing considerable offence to anybody who ever liked that song. In fact, a fellow musician and great friend of mine sitting near the stage had his head in his hands during the whole spectacle, but by this time I was too locked into trying to keep up the 5/4 rhythm, which I never found easy in the first place.

The fact is, when I listened to the original song later in Murph's car, the rhythm was so staggeringly easy to emulate that it seemed such an inappropriate drum application could only be entirely deliberate, which would explain the rather shocked and hurt expressions on the rest of the band's faces when we finally finished the song. They could only have concluded that they must have offended me in some unmentionably awful way and this was my way of getting them back.

One guy actually came up to me after the set and said: 'When you played "Cold Shot", at first I thought you were being incredibly clever. Then as you carried on I realised you had just completely fucked up!'

Usually experienced drummers are more than capable of picking up the groove of a song they've never heard before after a couple of bars, so most can sit in with an unrehearsed band if necessary. The problem is, other musicians tend to think this means that drumming is really easy and that the principle of 'play the intro and he'll get it' applies every time. Usually it does, but occasionally it's possible for a drummer to hear a riff or intro differently, so that he interprets the rhythm wrongly. When that happens, there is very little he can do about it, because his mind is locked into a certain time signature and he can't hear it any other way. Not unless you all stop and start again, which is embarrassing. So on that occasion I had to play the whole thing completely wrong like a real tosser all the way through.

Oh well, at least I managed to invent a new dance.

Of course, as Keith Moon proved almost on a daily basis, there are times when we deserve to be reprimanded...

SCRATCHWOOD SERVICES

Scratchwood. A gargantuan greasy spoon on the M1 motorway just north of London, now known as London Gateway Services. In the late '70s it became a kind of ritual for my band to stop in for a celebratory fry-up on the way back from our London gigs. It made us feel like we were a 'real' band on tour. In those days, Scratchwood Services was first and foremost the late-night domain of burly truck drivers. These people controlled huge vehicles for which you needed a special heavy goods licence and a tough, worldly countenance that befitted such an occupation.

Second in the pecking order were rock bands, and, a long way behind them, normal people. Drunken yobs were not generally in abundance because the truckers would not tolerate them. If you were young, intoxicated and wanted to engage in unarmed combat with a 90 per cent chance of coming out on top, Scratchwood was not the place to go. In short, big blokes don't like to be interrupted when they're shovelling their beans.

Of course, bands could be boisterous, especially after a boozy post-gig session, but truckers tended to regard musicians with a kind of distant tolerance, and we skin-beaters and chord-strummers very wisely accepted our inferior status. It was a bit like the relationship that exists between domestic dogs and cats.

Up to a point.

One night back in 1979, after a particularly inconsequential support gig in town, we dropped in for our customary fry-up and mug of builder's splosh. The band we'd been supporting had had a large amount of dry ice among their equipment, in the form of solid carbon dioxide stored in pint glasses, and our roadies had 'borrowed' several glasses of the stuff for possible future use.

Our arrival at Scratchwood was, technically, in the future. Or so I reasoned. Queuing up for some grub, I got some of the dry ice cubes and slipped a couple over the counter and into the trays from which the old dears served the food. The roadies soon got the gist of my plan and joined in.

The food counter at Scratchwood is very long, which turned out to be the perfect platform from which to conduct our experiment. The dry ice did what dry ice does when brought into contact with H_2O: it produced smoke. Lots of smoke. Ill-versed in the ways of special effects, it seemed we'd been somewhat over-enthusiastic as thick plumes of smoke cascaded over the food counter, soon covering the entire restaurant floor to a height of about four feet. It was like a Hammer horror film. Or an Ozzy Osbourne gig. A huge midnight café full of burly, tough-looking truckers eating beans on a *Top of the Pops* set not looking particularly happy about it. Those musician poofs had gone too far this time. Even the serving people behind the counter failed to see the funny side as they couldn't tell what they were scooping onto the plates.

Suddenly the doors burst open and a furious-looking manager marched in. I was for it. A night in the cells beckoned. The manager strode up to me, but just as I was about to protest that it was just a boyish prank that had gone too far, he burst out laughing. Thank God! His reaction placated the grumbling Neanderthals, who ended up grinning in vague amusement as the rock 'n' roll special effects continued to creep around their legs.

It would, actually, have made quite a good video.

THE RED LION

Tim Turan started out as a drummer in 1974 with his first band Llamedos (Sod 'Em All backwards). In 1979 he joined the popular London band The Car Thieves. He and I actually played on the same stage one night in Watford when The Car Thieves were sharing the bill with Sid Sideboard And The Chairs. These days he still plays drums for various outfits and also runs a mastering studio, Turan Audio, working with people such as Buzzcocks, Slade, Madness and The Osmonds. This story takes us back to October 1980.

My band, The Car Thieves, are playing at a big pub called The Red Lion in Bushey, just off the A41 near Watford. Personally, I don't like the place. Still, it's a gig. I walk past the huge Red Lion sign and into the separate function room/bar and set my drums up on the stage at the far end of the room. After a quick sound check, we retire to the saloon bar to wait for the crowd to turn up. As we look around the near empty bar, I comment on the bad taste of whoever designed the décor. Who in their right mind would put up pink wallpaper and then cover the floor in red lino?

People start to filter in and by 9pm it's quite packed. It's time for the band to get ready for show time in the function room, which is nearly full. To kick off tonight's performance, it has been decided by our band's leader, Paul Jensen, that I am to come on stage through the window at the back, dressed in a full suit of armour. That means the whole works: dressed head to toe as if I am about to go into battle for Henry VIII.

This means that I must put my armour on in the car park outside the pub, where I can be seen from the roundabout on the A41. I get some strange looks from passers by, presumably wondering just what's happening in the Red Lion. However, not all goes to plan. As I enter through the window, I catch the elbow of my suit on the heavy felt curtains, smash down onto my drum kit, head butt the mounted tom and kill my knees on the snare drum. But miraculously I land bum-first on the stool, so I scream '1-2-3-4!' through the visor to rapturous applause and off we go.

An hour's raunchy set ensues. During a break in the last number, we're getting the audience to clap along. For some reason, the band all pick up empty beer glasses and pretend to bring them together above our heads, as if using them to clap with. Some members of the audience copy this gesture. However, somewhat astonishingly, they actually make contact with the glasses, which begin to break. This craze seems to spread around the room and before long the floor is covered in broken glass. Then we stop playing and let the audience keep time with the beer glasses for a full three minutes!

When we come back in for the final chorus play-out, singer Paul takes it upon himself in all the excitement to leap off the stage and grab onto the big chandelier hanging in the middle of the room. The whole unit including the ceiling rose and all the surrounding plaster comes crashing down. The chandelier is now swinging two feet from the floor with audience members taking it in turns to push it back and forth like a huge swing, while glass ornaments fly all over the place. Paul clambers back on stage to wrap the show up.

After the gig, I am advised to leave the same way I came in, as the landlord wants to see me. He has lost several dozen beer glasses and his once lovely chandelier, and is very cross. And he's not very nice at the best of times, let alone when he's cross. So the bass player and myself leg it out of the window at the back.

On our way through the pub car park, we decide it might be a good idea to make a slight alteration to the huge pub sign at the front, which is made out of big individual wooden letters. All it takes is for me to get on the bass player's shoulders and swap two of the letters around. Pedro (our roadie) stands lookout as we perform our trickery.

Then, job done, we leave the pub car park with a squeal of tyres and blue smoke, charge up the road, surveying our handiwork as we depart. The sign now reads: The Red Lino.

GENERATION GAP

Gemma Clarke, drummer of The Krak and former drummer with Babyshambles, remembers her first big tour with the girl band The Suffragettes, and one of her first major recording sessions, during which she behaved like a very naughty girl.

The Suffragettes are on a support tour in America. It's my first ever tour and an exciting time for a young girl of 17. We've just been signed by Sony, which is why we've got the gig supporting '60s legends Vanilla Fudge. In fact, it's a strange situation because I am well under half the age of their drummer, whose name I can never remember ('Carmine' something or other).

During a break in the tour, our management decide that it's a good idea to record some tracks for a new album, so I find myself in a studio, laying down several takes of the first song. I'm still a little nervous. Recording is a different discipline from live playing and I find it difficult having to do take after take. It doesn't help when, every so often, someone keeps interrupting a take to give me advice over the headphones: 'Hit the crash cymbal at the end of the bar, not the beginning!'

The person giving me this advice from the control room is none other than the drummer with the headline band on the tour, whose name I keep forgetting. He's quite recognisable, though, as he has wild, black curly hair and a big black moustache. He seems friendly enough but he's of a much older generation and it's a bit like being told what to do by a tutor or an old uncle. Although I realise it's all good advice, it nevertheless irritates me that someone else is telling me how to play on my own song. And the longer it goes on, the bossier he seems to be getting. So the inevitable happens.

'Gemma, on that last bit you should try hitting...'

'Shut the f*** up! Who do you think you are? Stop trying to tell me how to play!'

The older guy gets the message and shuts up. I feel a bit bad because he was only trying to help and he's probably someone I could learn a lot from. I'm also a bit worried that I might get a telling off after the session.

But instead he seems perfectly friendly as we drive off to somewhere near the centre of town. 'I've got a surprise for you!' Soon we're approaching a huge warehouse-type building with a massive poster on the wall for the world to see. To my astonishment, the face on the poster is none other than the drummer escorting me in the car, the one with the wild black hair and moustache, and whose name I can never remember. Next to his face on the poster is written: Carmine Appice new drum store opening Saturday 9am.

So I'm being taken as a special guest to a grand drum store

opening by the owner, who is obviously quite a famous drummer. He escorts me into the new store, which seems even bigger on the inside. I look around in sheer wonderment at drum kits of every make and colour, racks of cymbals and accessories of every kind. It reminds me of when I was four years old and my dad took me into my first sweet shop. But my dad didn't say what Carmine says next: 'Choose anything you want. Anything at all!'

And so it was that Gemma Clarke, 17-year old drummer with The Suffragettes, was taken by the world famous Carmine Appice of Vanilla Fudge to his new drum store opening and told to choose anything she wanted – after she had effectively told him to where to go. Gemma chose a Peace drum kit in blue with Istanbul cymbals made by Avedis Zildjian, after which she was photographed with Carmine by the paparazzi.

Not bad for an afternoon's work and a quick studio tantrum.

SECTION 7

IT'S JUST A SCRATCH!

Drummers Are Superhuman...

Drummers tend to be the toughest member of the band. Or at least, playing the drums usually involves more physical exertion than, say, playing a guitar or keyboard. A degree of personal fitness and strength is generally considered fairly important if you are a working professional or even a semi-pro player in a local band.

But does that mean that a drummer's immune system should be streets ahead of anyone else's? Or that his/her body has a certain superhero quality when it comes to fast recovery from sudden injury? Apparently so...

No Pulling Sickies

Steve Grantley is drummer with both The Alarm and Stiff Little Fingers. He has also played with a number of top artists including Alicia Keys and Julian Lennon. Between juggling tours and recording, he has also found time to write two books: *The Who By Numbers*, which tells the story behind every Who song, and *Cum on, Feel the Noize*, a

MAD, BAD AND DANGEROUS

biography of Slade. I met Steve in The Crown and 2 Chairmen pub in London's Soho and he told me about a couple of incidents that further illustrate the levels of unshakable commitment we drummers are expected to adopt.

It's a full house at The Forum, Kentish Town. Steve is due on-stage to play to a couple of thousand people as drummer with Stiff Little Fingers. The atmosphere is charged and it should be a good gig. There's one little problem, however. Steve can hardly stand up. He is, in fact, in a very poor state.

The night before I'd been very ill with some kind of virus which had been threatening for days. I had the emergency doctor out at three in the morning and he gave me morphine and suggested I take a week off as I was exhausted. There was no chance of that – we had a gig the next night and cancelling the show 'just because the drummer feels a bit rough' was out of the question.

I went on stage in a daze that night. I was glad to sit down on the drum throne because I was about to fall over. How I got through the gig I'll never know but the band were less than understanding. Their only comment after my valiant attempt to keep going despite my condition? 'It was a bit slow in places.'

Yeah right, come on Steve – we know you felt a bit dicky but you let the side down, man! What's the worst illness you can imagine having to cope with while playing the drums live in front of thousands of people? Laryngitis? Food poisoning? Shingles? As it turned out, in Steve's case it was pneumonia.

But cancel a gig? Nah. Tub-thumpers just gotta get on with it, right?

ADRENALINE: BETTER THAN ANY DRUG

Ian Mosley is the highly acclaimed drummer with prog rock band Marillion. He joined the band in 1984, prior to which he had played with an assortment of big names such as guitarist Gordon Giltrap and ex-Genesis guitarist Steve Hackett. He also released a solo album, *Crossing the Desert*, in 1996.

I met Ian in a hotel bar in Tring, Hertfordshire, where he had been recording a new album. There we touched upon the business of drummers being expected to have superhuman powers of recovery when inflicted with illness or injury.

I'd been wandering along a street in Streatham daydreaming about my forthcoming tour of the US with Steve Hackett. Rehearsals had been going well and we were leaving in five days. I was feeling a little peckish so I decided to pop into a small restaurant for a bite to eat. Four days later I was in hospital. Apparently I had been served an unthawed chicken and a vile and sinister culture had grown in my intestine. I am not supposed to leave hospital.

Although I'm feeling pretty ill, I decide to discharge myself.

To be fair, drummers do tend to have a kind of rugged determination to carry on against all odds. And if you're prepared to display that kind of courage then other people, like band members, agents or roadies, are only too pleased to encourage it, as though they knew all along that you couldn't really be that ill.

So having walked out of hospital and got on his flight, Ian is about to do a sound check at the first show of the tour, in Cleveland.

I'm about to do the sound check. The problem is, I can hardly stand up. Chas Cronk, our bass player, holds me up as I walk on stage to the drums. I flop down onto my drum stool and we begin to play. As I'm going round the kit I start to get really dizzy. I can't believe I'm actually attempting to do this at all. It all seems a bit surreal. The strange thing is, no one else seems to notice, and so the playing must be OK.

Unbelievably, when it came to showtime Ian managed to play the whole gig perfectly well. Not only that, the rest of the tour went fine although he was hardly able to eat a thing. However, Ian wasn't let off that lightly.

I'm waking up in my bed at home feeling unbelievably shattered. There's a strange man sitting beside me. As I come round he says: 'I'm Dr Foskit from the hospital.'

On arriving back in England Ian had once again taken very ill. The doctor was called and Ian had to spend several days on antibiotics recovering from severe food poisoning that simply would not go away. Ian reckons his body had deployed a series of controlled adrenaline rushes in order to get through each show on the tour. But when he got home and that was no longer necessary, he really paid the price. But that isn't the only incident in which Ian has displayed a typical drummer's courage.

I'm sitting in my hotel room in Stockholm with our tour manager. Tonight we're playing to 7000 people at The Globe theatre. And I'm feeling awful. I've been pissing razor blades and I've got a horrendous ear infection. Our tour manager receives a call from the venue. In the background I can hear the muted voice of our manager coming through his walkie-talkie. We are clearly having a three-way conversation.

Manager: 'How is he?'

Tour manager: 'Pretty bad I'm afraid.'

Manager: 'Oh dear, poor fellow. But listen, don't let him think we can cancel the show!'

Me: 'I heard that, you bastard...'

All very jovial, but the manager was perfectly serious. Another shining example of the consensus that drummers are a breed of people who simply are not allowed to be ill – at least not to an extent that would lead to spoiling things for everybody else.

THE SHOW MUST GO ON

Steve Phypers is drummer with The Overtures, the UK's most popular '60s covers band. They recently opened for Elton John at The O2 on New Year's Eve and were hired as the band for his wedding to David Furnish in 2005.

Steve is the best Keith Moon impersonator I have ever seen. Why? Because he's not a Keith Moon impersonator. He is a total natural. Certainly, he loves The Who and Moonie's drumming, but the faces he pulls and the mannerisms he incorporates while playing occur without deliberation, and his drumming (which is excellent) just happens to be of a similar style. But the really clever thing is, while Mr Moon created an erratic but somehow controlled mayhem that suited The Who's musical structure perfectly, Mr Phypers manages to incorporate this style into a set of mainly non-

Who numbers in such a way as to add a new dimension, without sacrificing an ounce of respect for the songs themselves, or indeed, the other performers in the band.

He also tells me that he never suffers from pre-gig nerves or jitters, which was also probably true of Moon. However, Steve's drumming life has not been without its memorable incidents, one of which is worth a mention as it serves as a useful example of the more unpleasant ordeals that can be experienced by us reliable guys at the back.

I'm on the deck of the *QE2*, probably the most prestigious cruise ship in the world. Destination: New York. I'm looking forward to my first ever gig as a drummer on a cruise liner. The Overtures have been booked on the strength of our reputation as first class musicians who deliver a first rate set, packed full of '60s and '70s classics: Beatles to Yardbirds, Kinks to Walker Brothers. The ship's auditorium is fully booked for this evening's performance, which is a good sign. The rest of the band are resting in their cabins and as the sun's gone in and the sea's getting a bit choppy, I figure it might be a good idea to take a stroll below decks and while away the next few hours before it's time to sound check.

I get up from my sun lounger and start strolling. Suddenly, without warning, a startlingly unpleasant sensation grips my insides. Almost immediately I am consumed with a feeling of intense nausea. I grip the railings to steady myself. Then it comes: the unstoppable, seismic surge from the well of the stomach that is the manifest result of severe sea sickness. I have no choice but to go with it. And it's relentless. At least there's plenty of sea to be sick into, because this obviously isn't going to go away for a while.

The band's sound engineer happens to pass by and, observing my predicament expresses concern that I should be all sicked out and OK for this evening's performance. I point out that funnily enough the very same thought had occurred to me a while back. But hey, everyone has to get their kicks somehow! Still, in spite of the fun I'm having honking my heart out over the side of the QE2, I promise to do my very best to get this sordid little incident out of the way before tea time.

I eventually make it back to my cabin and other members of the band and crew are beginning to show some genuine concern for my wellbeing, because, at the end of the day, the show must go on. We're all in the middle of the ocean, so getting a replacement drummer or even a band is not an option.

As luck would have it, the choppy seas eventually calm and my sickness subsides. The soundman expresses great relief but still looks a little worried as we wait in the wings before taking the stage. There is a short film set to music scheduled as an intro to the band and I am standing with the rest of the guys waiting for this to begin – which doesn't happen. After a while, the audience begins to get agitated by the lack of entertainment and a slow handclap starts.

The floor manager appears at the other side of the wings and beckons the band onto the stage. This is embarrassment indeed, walking on stage to a slow handclap. But as I sit down at my drum kit, I notice something far worse: the bass drum pedal has chosen this moment to play its ugliest trick of all.

Somehow, even though I tightened it with my special drummer's Allen key, the beater has come loose and fallen through the hole. That would imply that the thread on the screw has gone, which means replacing the drum pedal with a spare, which is back stage.

Still, I bend down and try and refasten the beater, trying not to think about the fact that I'm in front of a capacity audience on the *QE2* on the way to New York, trying to rectify a technical problem to the sound of a slow hand clap orchestrated by a gathering of people who have all paid a lot of money to be here.

Meanwhile, the sound man is panicking even more, because, from where he's sitting, it looks very much as though my earlier sickness has returned as I appear to be bent double, vomiting behind my drum kit…

Eventually The Overtures walked off stage to a standing ovation at the end of the gig which, according to the ship's captain, was a first on the *QE2*. So it goes to show that vomit and bastard bass drum pedals don't necessarily have to spoil the bigger picture.

Steve's illness was the result of unavoidable circumstances – unlike the physical sickness that engulfed a drummer friend of mine, Mark (Charlie) Sugden. However, he still displayed the same determination not to let it spoil things.

The band was The Harper Brothers. The tour was the French Alps around Ser Chevalier and Chant Merle. The idea was to ski during the day and gig at night. But not before hitting the après ski with some gusto.

On this particular occasion Charlie was seated behind his kit at a place called Jack's Bar. Prior to this, he had been bouncing around in a rickety van up 23 hairpin bends, on top of a heavy après-ski session, to reach the summit of the highest mountain in the resort. During the first number, it all got too much for him and he projectile vomited while playing. But, like a true professional, he turned his head and directed the spray stage left, expertly missing his kit and with such precision as to avoid his hi-hat. And he didn't miss a beat.

SOLDIERING ON

Steve Dixon's first notable band was FBI back in the mid-'70s, a well-known soul/funk outfit signed to RCA Records. They made one album before folding, after which he toured Australia with a chart-topping band, Supercharge, for six weeks, about which he remembers very little. Then came an even bigger break when he joined the disco singers The Real Thing, appearing on *Top of the Pops* and supporting the likes of David Essex on tour. More recently Steve has played with Ray Davies and Kent-born New Orleans-style piano player Jon Cleary, which he particularly loved doing.

Steve is now Gary Moore's drummer and I caught up with him just after their European tour in autumn 2009. As ever, we were in a Soho pub. Somewhat coincidentally, on discussing our favourite drum moments, we discovered that we had the same favourite: when Ringo brings the drums in for the first time on 'Hey Jude'. We also touched upon this business about drummers soldiering on when injured and he told me this story...

Tonight the Gary Moore band is due to play the Heineken Music Hall in Amsterdam. I'm walking along after dinner when suddenly I slip on the wet pavement. My reaction is to put my hand out to break the fall, something you should never do if you're a drummer. I feel a crack and a sharp pain but think little of it. After all, I can't afford to let the band and 5000 paying punters down. So I say nothing about it and carry on with the gig. It hurts a bit but seems mostly OK. I suspect it's another case of adrenaline to the rescue. Drummers seem to have a capacity to produce enough hormones to subdue any amount of pain temporarily.

The next morning I wake up in agony. My wrist is massively swollen and looks like a yellow and black rugby ball. So it's straight down to the hospital, where it's confirmed that I have a broken arm, which is put in a cast. Luckily, we have a break in the tour and our next gig is in three weeks' time, so I'm thinking I might be better by then. Fat chance. My arm improves only slightly. Nevertheless, I'm determined to do the rest of the tour and ask the good doctors at the hospital to remove my cast, which they are not happy about. They say it simply hasn't healed enough. When I explain my position they remove it but refuse to treat me if it gets more seriously damaged as a result.

I then buy a removable cast with a Velcro strip so I can take it off before each gig and some serious painkillers, plus some whisky – for medicinal purposes of course.

We resume the tour. On the second night I'm walking to the dressing room with Gary and begin to take off my cast. On hearing the Velcro rip he looks down and sees my injured arm for the first time. 'What's that?'

'Oh, I broke my arm a while back...'

'But why didn't you tell me? It looks awful."

Steve tells me that Gary was most concerned. It's an irony that the one time when a bandleader actually is sympathetic to a drummer's injury, the drummer has already decided to carry on regardless. Notice how Steve didn't even consider the option of telling Gary Moore or any of the others. It's as though a drummer's in-built instinct is to make as little fuss as possible.

It certainly seems to be the case that drummers have an in-built determination not to let the rest of the band down. At the risk of sounding like a brand-marketing freak, it's in our DNA. Nigel Glockler from Saxon tells me that during one tour he actually had to be carried on stage in a wheelchair...

We were on tour in the States with Cheap Trick when I felt a cold coming on. As soon as that happens I get out the remedies, dose myself up and sweat it out. However after a week of this I was still feeling crap. Eventually I felt so low I asked to see a doctor and ended up at a hospital being told I had acute pneumonia. I was told not to play under any circumstances. Being pig-headed, I pleaded with the doctor to dose me up and let me play as I didn't want the band to have to cancel the rest of the tour. Eventually he relented, as long as I stayed in bed the rest of the time.

I went back to the venue and found that Bun E Carlos, Cheap Trick's drummer, had very kindly offered to sit in. But as he didn't know the songs it was decided that I would carry on as best I could, so I was wheelchaired to the stage and wore an oxygen mask for the gig. I could only play the rhythms – I didn't have enough energy to do a lot of fills – but we got through it.

I wore an oxygen mask for the next load of gigs and gradually improved. But I was still pissed off that I had to stay in bed during the day, feeling like I had a bayonet sticking in my lungs, while the guys were sunbathing and swimming! When I got home, because I was so run down I contracted Bell's Palsy. Oh joy!

Whether deliberately or under protest, performing under considerably unpleasant circumstances seems to be an integral part of any drummer's lot in life. Not only due to illness or injury sustained before a performance, but also while actually playing. Steve Grantley told me about an especially painful experience he suffered on stage at at The Academy in Manchester with Stiff Little Fingers.

As with many drummers, I leave a small pile of sawdust, from the stick hitting the hi-hat, by my left foot. However, four songs before the end of the gig, a large chunk of wood from the stick flew straight into my eye. This wasn't a splinter – it was a chunk. Now, these final four songs all ran into each other so I couldn't stop. I had to play on with a big lump of wood sticking in my eye.

When I came off stage I asked my trusted tech, Jonesy, to 'Get this f***ing thing outta my f***ing eye!' He cringed, took a deep breath and pulled the wood from my watering, bloody eye. The relief was so beautiful, I said, 'Cheers, mate' and went straight back on to do the encore!

Miraculously Steve was unharmed. The nature of our instrument means we are more likely to be at risk of random injury, but even when we are targeted for deliberate injury, our resilience and determination to carry on is often beyond the call of duty...

ROUGH TREATMENT

Adam Ficek joined Babyshambles in 2005, having previously played with The White Sport and Mains Ignition. He has also recorded a second album with his other project, Roses Kings Castles, which was produced by Smiths and Blur producer Stephen Street. Adam told me about an unfortunate episode that occurred when Babyshambles were in the middle of an Italian tour.

We are playing The Piper Room, a historic Italian venue in Rome. The sound check goes well and before long the place is packed and it's show time. Towards the middle of the set, I'm playing away happily on a particular favourite Babyshambles song of mine. Just as we are reaching the song's outro, I feel a blinding crack on my nose. Searing pain envelopes my face and head, then everything goes black.

The next thing I know I'm waking up back in the dressing room. Someone is gently dabbing my face with a wet flannel. I am covered in blood. I can even see stars. But I can't remember a thing. In fact I can barely remember who I am. I spend what seems like ages staring blankly ahead, dazed and in a lot of pain.

'What the hell happened?' I ask. Apparently a fan hurled a bottle of fine Italian red wine at me. A full bottle.

Our bass player is standing over me looking concerned. How sweet, I'm thinking. But it turns out he's worried that the band won't be able to finish the gig, so could I manage to go back on and play a few more songs...

'...please?'

The show finishes and I'm relieved to have got through the last bit. My face and head are still throbbing as the band arrive back at the hotel. To my dismay there are loads of paparazzi pushing and shoving as we try and make it to the entrance. A scrap develops. Next thing I know I'm on the ground, rolling round with the rest of the band scuffling with overzealous Italian paps.

Eventually the police are called and we make it into the hotel. I go straight to bed as I'm feeling a bit queasy. As I'm drifting off to sleep, I'm trying to think of the title of the song we were playing when that bottle hit me. Ahh yes... 'Sedative'.

So, to recap, the drummer receives a substantial injury which renders him confused and in agony. But instead of taking him to the nearest A&E department to make sure he's not suffering from concussion or worse, the band twist his arm (so to speak) to get him to be a brave boy and finish the set. Which, had he been concussed, would have been even more dangerous.

Drummers always seem to be the victims of physical abuse. But why is it that for some reason we are expected to take it all in our stride, as if being a drummer means one is automatically blessed with a significantly higher pain threshold? It's as though our chosen instrument indicates a lesser degree of sensitivity, which is accompanied by a greater natural resilience to rough treatment.

Pretty well every drummer I spoke to has had to play under extreme conditions. Top US session man Lee Levin tells me he once played a week backing Julio Iglesias at Caesar's Palace in Las Vegas with a really bad virus. 'I had to play every night with a pail next to the drums just in case I needed to throw up.'

Nice. The difficult bit would be desperately wanting to throw up but having to hold it in until the end of the song. And then, when you've finally launched yourself at the bowl and had a good old puke, you look up to see everyone is waiting for you to start the next song. Then you're thinking, 'Hang on – shall I try and throw up some more just in case?'

The point is, for a drummer to throw up during a song is not ideal. The violent jerking of someone who is being really ill is likely, in no small measure, to influence his ability to deliver an effortlessly smooth and steady drum groove. Quite apart from which, the clientele at Caesar's Palace in Las Vegas would surely not wish to be treated to the sight of a drummer throwing up all over his hi-hat. Worse still, it might be seen as a reflection on Julio himself.

'To all the girls I've loved before...'

Cue the puking drummer.

Lee had a similar experience in Guatemala, only this time he had caught a really nasty stomach bug causing terrible diarrhoea, so the problem was at the other end. The show was in Guatemala City in front of three to five thousand people.

I'm not sure how close I actually came to defecating on my appropriately titled drum 'throne'. What I do remember is that it wasn't much of an issue as long as I was actually playing. But as soon as I would stop, that desperate feeling would come back. Had there been an acoustic moment in the show where I could break away, the audience would have seen the drummer make a run for it pretty sharpish.

To make matters worse, the show actually ended with the band filing off stage one by one, waving to the audience, leaving me to do an extended drum solo...

That must have been the shortest drum solo ever. But the human body, especially that of a drummer, has an amazing capacity for suspending certain crucially pending needs for as long as is humanly possible.

When I met Woody from Madness he told me how he had spent one gig in Belfast vomiting before and during the show, even chucking up violently after each encore. Apparently he had a severe fever with a temperature of over 100 degrees due to gastric flu. He was so bad he had to play trussed up in a thick bomber jacket, shivering all the way through. You've got to be very resilient to do a full on show in that condition.

But even when we drummers are not suffering from illness or injury, we still have to be generally pretty fit, and Woody is no exception...

ONE MORE TIME PLEASE

Woody (Dan Woodgate) was brought up in London's Camden Town. His dad was a photographer to the stars, taking pictures of people like Peter Cook, Albert Finney, John Hurt and Joanna Lumley. His brother Nick took up the guitar and Woody joined in by playing along on anything he could find, be it cushions, sofas or the piano stool.

Soon Woody and his mates were jamming at parties in and around Camden. Then bass player Mark Bedford introduced him to a recently formed ska pop group called Madness. Quite a timely introduction, as shortly after joining the band they became an overnight sensation. The band's unique visual presentation of their songs became part of their trademark and is as fun and stimulating today as it was 30 years ago. Since 1987, Woody has also played with Voice Of The Beehive, but continues to be with Madness.

I managed to meet with Woody just as he'd come off a British tour. We met a few days before Christmas upstairs in a private room at a great pub called The Harp, near Covent Garden. He told me how Madness had always enjoyed a good relationship with the boys in Oasis.

We're doing this festival in Paris – two stages in two separate fields, A and B. Oasis are headlining on the A stage and we've got the spot before them on the B stage. We'd prefer to be on the A stage but Oasis have insisted we play on the B.

The gig goes really well. All our fans are up for a party and they go berserk, which is what we're all about. We finish our second encore, 'Nightboat to Cairo', and make our way, knackered and sweaty back to our dressing room. We're sitting around, having a drink/fag/sandwich/generally winding down when we realise something's not quite right.

Gem, the second guitarist with Oasis, hasn't come in to see us. He always makes a point of coming in for a chat when we're doing gigs together. But today there's no sign of him. After a while the gig's promoter comes into the dressing room and announces that Oasis have split. They're not appearing tonight. Then he asks if we can stand in for them. OK, we might be a bit knackered but the management and promoters would really appreciate our help.

I suppose if you're going to ask a band to play a full set twice in succession, it might as well be Madness. But they must have been worried about the fact that Oasis fans had paid to see Oasis and the Madness fans had already just seen them, sung along, danced and jumped and generally gone mad. They've already peaked, so to speak. Plus they must have been exhausted. Madness music isn't exactly backroom jazz – it's high-energy stuff that builds audiences into a frenzy. What is also notable here is the lack of consideration for the fact that playing the drums in particular is a pretty tiring business. But it didn't faze Woody...

But hey, at the end of the day we're Madness, so why not? So about an hour later we are announced once more, this time on the A stage. What amazes us is that the crowd go completely crazy. There's nobody left in the B field, so we're playing to a combination of Oasis fans plus all the people who've already seen us. But they're all just as up for it as they were before. We do an hour's set and finish the show.

So Madness eventually got to play both A and B stages, one after the other to equally ecstatic crowds. Good for them. Especially Woody, who has proved once again how much energy and stamina a drummer actually needs to possess as a matter of course. Did it bother him playing the same show twice?

No, not really...

I reckon they should contact the Guinness Book of Records, It must be the longest encore in history.

While talking to Rob Franks, drummer with popular Madness tribute band Badness, I discovered a particularly unpleasant example of a drummer playing under duress...

Imagine you are watching your favourite Madness tribute band at a large London club venue. The band is great, doing all the usual, jerky dance moves that made the real Madness such distinctive performers. Then you look at the drummer.

For some reason, his mouth is wide open and he is salivating. So much so that thick spittle is dribbling like an ever-flowing waterfall down his chin. He looks like he's gone completely mad. He doesn't seem to want to shut his mouth at all. He just keeps on salivating and dribbling throughout the whole show.

You figure it must be something to do with drugs. Not so. Rob Franks, the drummer in question, was suffering from an extremely severe attack of gingivitis and his gums were so badly swollen that he couldn't shut his mouth. Nor could he swallow because the inflammation had caused an infection at the back of his throat. Apparently they call it Gob Rot. I think we'll leave it there.

Suffice to say that drummers are, in the main, fiercely determined people. Perhaps the ultimate example is Rick Allen, Def Leppard's drummer, who has continued to play with a specially adapted kit after losing his left arm in a car accident in 1984.

SECTION 8

SECTION 3

EXPECT THE UNEXPECTED

A Drummer's Life Is Full Of Surprises...

During my research I was led to the conclusion that a drummer can expect to be involved in some very bizarre incidents. Naturally, odd things can happen to you whatever instrument you play, but it seems to be in the fundamental nature of a drummer's persona to expect to encounter some truly weird stuff.

BROTHERLY LOVE

In 1983, a fresh-faced 17-year-old went to an audition for an unnamed band. The band turned out to be The Style Council and the drummer was Steve White, who was asked back the next day. Steve stayed with the band for many years and went on to play on Paul Weller's solo albums as well as drumming with a host of people like Ian Dury, The Who and Oasis. He was also the youngest person to take the stage at Live Aid in 1985. Twenty-four years and 15 million-selling albums later, he remains one of Britain's most gifted and influential drummers.

I met Steve just outside Footes' famous drum store in London's Golden Square. We took a stroll to a nearby Pizza Express where we chatted a good deal about what it means to be a drummer. I particularly liked this story.

It's 2001 and I'm not doing a lot as Paul is writing the next album. I receive a call from Noel Gallagher of Oasis. Apparently their drummer, who happens to be my brother Alan, has sustained an injury and had to pull out of their next US tour, which starts in about a week. It's short notice, but can I step in? I'm one of the few guys the band can trust to get it together at such short notice. He emphasises that the tour is a bit special as the headline spots are to be shared with The Black Crowes, who are huge in the States. It's billed as The Brotherly Love tour.

Of course I'd love to do it but as I work for Paul, it's courtesy to check with him first. I call Paul who says there's not much planned for the next few months that can't be shifted, so go for it! I call Noel back and say I'm up for it. He's really pleased and tells the others in the room: 'Whitey's up for it!'

As this happens, a huge black crow falls from the sky and lands on the grass on the front lawn through the window in front of me. It flaps around for a while and then dies in front of my eyes. This unnerves me and momentarily I lose concentration on my telephone call. The crow is now motionless and I relay what I've just seen to the elder Gallagher on the other end of the line, who then tells the band: 'Fuckin' hell, a big black crow has just crashed and died in front of Whitey in his garden.'

There's a bit of a silence. Then I hear Liam Gallagher's

voice down the line: 'Tell him it's great he can do the tour but he's not fookin' flying with us!'

The tension is broken and talk begins of songs and rehearsals and the tour to come. All goes well and sure enough, a week later the flights have been booked and we're all off to the States for the Brotherly Love tour.

Oasis are flying Virgin.

And I'm flying BA.

CANINE CRITIC

Jazz drummer Eddie Clayton started playing gigs in the late 1940s while still at school. He then had two years in the RAF, playing side drum and kit in the Station Band at RAF Lyneham, and drums with The Skyliners RAF band at Swindon Locarno ballroom. After discharge from the RAF he had a stint with The Fred Hedley Big Band, before running his own 16-piece Big Band through the 1950s. After that he concentrated on his Trio and Quartet, playing the usual round of clubs and private functions. Many of the top names in UK jazz have appeared as guests with Eddie's band since the 1970s: Jimmy Skidmore, Tommy Whittle, Kenny Baker, Enrico Tomasso and Alan Barnes, to mention a few.

I met Eddie in his local pub and he told me about an incident some years ago.

I'm playing in a small jazz combo in the music bar at the Red Lion pub on the A41 bypass near Bushey, Watford. My son, Leon, is on bass. We arrive a bit early, so we have a drink at the bar. Ken the landlord comes over, says hello and introduces us to his dog, also called Leon.

As we're setting up, Leon comments on the fact that I have cut a large hole in the front skin of my bass drum. I explain that it's become general practice for a lot of drummers, because it's useful for accommodating microphones at bigger gigs and pillows or cushions to deaden the sound. I then place a small, newly laundered cushion in my bass drum.

The gig goes fairly well and we are met with a fairly warm reception. During our last number Leon the dog appears and saunters up onto the small stage. We carry on playing, hoping he'll get bored and go away.

But he doesn't. Instead he eases himself bum-first into my bass drum, stays there for a short while and then leaves the stage. The punters at the front are in hysterics. I can see the ones further back near the bar craning their heads to see what all the fuss is about.

After we finish the song to over-exaggerated applause and whoops of laughter, Leon takes a look inside my bass drum. Then he turns to me and says: 'Apparently you were crap tonight.'

PEACH MOON

Years ago I would never decline an offer to play drums for one-off gigs or even long term projects. I always felt flattered to be asked. More importantly, there was always this underlying fear that the one gig I turned down would turn out to be the one that lead to that once-in-a-lifetime opportunity to make it. Even if the chances were ridiculously remote, it seemed fundamentally wrong to say no.

On one occasion, however, I escaped a gig at the last minute that could not have been less likely to enhance my reputation as a drummer. I had just finished a gig with a band called The Giants, at a pub in Radlett in Hertfordshire, when a hippyish fellow approached me and asked if I'd like to play with his band for one gig.

It was to be on the back of a flat bed truck at the Radlett Festival a couple of weeks away. It sounded like fun (and of course, you never knew what promoters of considerable repute might be attending the event) so I said yes. We agreed that he would let me have a tape to listen to beforehand as opposed to rehearsing, which naturally suited me. The tape was to arrive in the post in good time for me to familiarise myself with their material.

During the next few days I mostly put it out of my mind, although occasionally I mused on the possible advantages of gaining some more local notoriety in Radlett, for purposes of pure vanity. However, the tape did not arrive. By the morning of the event I had assumed the whole idea had either fizzled out or they'd found someone else. In a sense I was relieved because I could get on with the usual Saturday business of going down the pub to see all my friends.

As I was coming downstairs to have breakfast in happy anticipation of this, I saw a package on the doormat. My heart sank. I had got used to the idea of spending the day at leisure, and by now I had become suspicious about the whole affair. Sure enough, it turned out to be the promised tape, on which was written the name of the band: Peach Moon. My brother-in-law at the time, Chris Neale (a very fine musician and songwriter), happened to be at our house and we listened to the tape together.

We could not believe our ears. What we heard was so

atrocious that it defies description in conventional terms, but I will try. There was vague evidence of an out-of-tune acoustic guitar, perhaps accompanied by another, although we could not quite tell. No other musical instruments were apparent on the recording, which also featured a man slurring a series of pretentious phrases. The sentiments contained therein were articulated with a kind of giggly snarl, as though he had happened upon some ultimate utopian planet on which existed all that could conceivably be desirable to man but made available only to him. The arrogance was so astonishing, especially considering the absence of any musical ability, that in a sense it was brilliant.

I wondered if perhaps I had been sent the wrong tape, or possibly the original material had been recorded over by a mad person. So I decided to ring my musician friend, Paul Jensen (whose band I was in at the time), who lived in Radlett and was likely to be attending the festival, to ask if he had heard of them.

Luckily, he was at home. On mentioning the name Peach Moon, there followed a long silence, which was broken by Paul saying in a very serious, almost pleading voice: 'Spike, if you do perform with these people on the back of that truck, would you please make sure you don't talk to me or any of my friends before or afterwards. I would really appreciate it if you kept away from us. Nothing personal, I just feel it would be for the best.'

I had my answer. But it was too late, for as I put the phone down a car drew up outside the house. It was a Citroën, loaded with a pile of guitars and drums etc, all without cases and seemingly poking out of every orifice the car possessed.

The gentleman who had offered me the gig came towards the front door, followed by his girlfriend. I let them into our back garden (it was a sunny day) where I introduced them to my sister. I later discovered that the girlfriend used to bully my sister in the toilets at school. She had obviously undergone some kind of moral conversion since then. My sister went to make them some coffee – and no, she's not the type to spit in it, but boy was there an opportunity for vengeance.

Anyway, I digress. I had to get out of that gig. So I went into the house for five minutes and returned to the garden looking as surprised and dismayed as possible. You'll never believe it, I explained, but that was Sid Sideboard's manager on the phone. He's booked the studio for us to record the follow-up to our current single 'Bucket & Spade' this afternoon! I'm so sorry, but I just can't play the Radlett festival after all!

Seeing the look of worry and disappointment on their faces I had more than a pang of guilt, so I gave them the number of a drummer friend who lived round the corner. He has not spoken to me since.

SECTION 9

A COMPLICATED BUSINESS

There's A Lot More To A Drummer Than Meets The Eye...

Drumming involves the whole person in as much as you need to have a degree of universal co-ordination, especially between mind and body. And as a fully co-ordinated piece of machinery, the drummer is responsible for shaping and maintaining the series of rhythmic patterns that provide the backbone of any form of beat music. In fact, there are several scientific mysteries/theories which help explain a little more about what makes us so special...

MUSCLE MEMORY

Sometimes, when I'm playing the drums at a gig, a feeling of blind panic unexpectedly overwhelms me. Suddenly I'm thinking: 'Oh no! How do I do this? What if I suddenly forget how to play the drums?' The feeling only lasts for a moment or so, but it's really frightening. I tend to force myself away from these thoughts: 'Stop thinking that way! Don't even go there...'

A drum kit is a complex apparatus and as a drummer you

are the machine that operates it. The whole business of limb co-ordination, levels of attack, volume dynamics, creative musical technique and sheer stamina is actually quite a challenge. What's more, it's one you have to rise to all the time. There are rarely opportunities to sit out and take a breather.

As a guitarist, if you get the panics you can perhaps strum your way quietly through it for a couple of bars and then carry on. But the drums are such an essential cog in the musical machine that you simply have to be on the money the whole time. If you falter even for a few seconds, chances are the whole thing will fall apart. So it's not surprising that it gets a bit scary if you think about it too much.

I used to think this kind of disorientation was simply part of my own peculiar sense of insecurity, until I met Woody from Madness. I discovered that he and many other drummers occasionally suffer the same experience.

The trick is to lock your mind into a level of concentration that allows you to forget about the repetitive nature of what you are doing by thinking of something else (like what you're having for dinner tomorrow) while remaining ultimately focussed on the overall effect of what you're doing. In fact, the brain has a fundamental feature that does this automatically. It's called 'muscle memory'. It's part of the brain's suite of tools, which give us the ability to consign certain repetitive activities to memory so that they become automatic. These are also known as 'motor skills'.

'Fine' motor skills are for everyday things like cleaning your teeth and washing your hands, whereas 'gross' motor skills come into action when you are doing things like playing a sport, driving a car or – yes, you've guessed it – playing the drums. So it's not surprising that the thought of it not working is pretty scary.

Imagine you are at a Christmas cocktail party enjoying the buffet and politely chatting to some neighbours. You have selected a piece of quiche and a couple of mushroom vol au vents. Mike and Barbara from next door come over and ask what you're doing on Christmas Day. All of a sudden your muscle memory stops working and you forget how to eat. Pastry starts to fall out of your mouth while the vol au vent filling is now dribbling down your chin.

You panic while trying to answer their question, which has a knock-on effect and you forget how to talk. The result is a gibbering wreck of a person who is apparently completely unable to deal with the simplest task in social discourse. And you know you won't be invited back next year.

The point is, when you're doing everyday things like eating or talking, your muscle memory is in constant use, allowing you to get on with your day without thinking of every detail of each little task. Even driving a car deploys this mind tool. In fact, if it were not for muscle memory the world would be full of people stumbling around, falling down stairs, banging into walls and generally behaving as though they are completely plastered. Drivers would be wearing permanent expressions of complete terror. And so would drummers.

However, playing the drums is a bit special. The activity occupies a space which, while being a necessary user of muscle memory, is not regarded by the brain as everyday activity. So sometimes it's open to question. Apparently, golfers suffer from the same occasional tendency to question what they are doing, and it makes them forget how to putt. In golfing parlance, it's called the yips.

Woody sometimes gets an attack of yips while playing a particular drum fill in the Madness song 'Baggy Trousers'. 'Ninety-nine per cent of the time I can play that song perfectly well all the way through,' says Woody. 'But, very occasionally, for some reason my body won't let me do a particular fill that features in part of the bridge part that starts with "Oh what fun we had…"'

It would have been particularly difficult to disguise because Madness songs are by nature quirky and the arrangements are very distinctive, so the audience is more likely to be aware of how each drum fill should go.

It seems this tendency to panic is fairly common. During my chat with Andy Burrows, erstwhile drummer with Razorlight before joining American indie rock act We Are Scientists, he revealed that he suffered really badly from it and had always wondered what it was. 'It often happens when I know there's a certain fill or tricky section coming up. Sometimes it's as though I'm gripping the sticks so hard I can hardly play. But I can honestly say I've never dropped a stick, missed a beat or messed up a roll. But it's not always a joyous experience.'

Apparently he has only suffered from this occasional lapse in muscle memory since he joined Razorlight. In fact, while on tour with Muse he even mentioned it to their drummer, Dominic Howard, who said he'd experienced it too. So I feel it's appropriate officially to name this condition for drummers as Drummer's Yips, and as such this shall be recognised as another reason to encourage a greater respect for the successful mastering of the art.

Sometimes Andy's sense of impending memory seizure extended beyond the act of drumming to conducting interviews, but only in Japan. He would suddenly get up and leave the room. This would probably have left the Japanese interview hosts more than a little confused. After all, Japanese culture embraces a particularly rigid social protocol involving much deep bowing of heads and torsos whenever anyone enters or leaves a room. But hey, that's rock'n'roll.

THE MAGIC OF THE GOLDEN RATIO

Bear with me a for a while. Ever since man began to seek more from his existence than mere survival, his adventures have afforded him discoveries of immeasurable quantity. One of these is known as the Golden Ratio: a scientific notion that a certain condition, arrived at by a combination of mathematic equations, can create a sense of complete satisfaction and well being.

Technically speaking, if you divide a line into two parts so that the longer part divided by the smaller part is also equal to the whole length divided by the longer part, then you will have achieved the Golden Ratio.

In mathematics and the arts, two quantities are in the Golden Ratio if the ratio of the sum of the quantities to the larger quantity is equal to the ratio of the larger quantity to the smaller one. This is also known as the Golden Section.

Ancient Greeks studied the theory as it frequently appeared in geometry. In more modern times, architects and artists have applied the proportions inherent in the Golden Ratio to their work.

This is best illustrated by what is known as the Golden Rectangle, in which the ratio of the longer side to the shorter side represents the Golden Ratio and, as such, is aesthetically pleasing. This pleasing mathematical equilibrium is thought also to manifest itself in certain musical passages and arrangements, and even individual drum patterns.

What a load of old bollocks, you might think.

Mind you, why do we like our front doors between two windows? Why does red go with yellow and not with purple? And why do we sing along to 'Hi-Ho Silver Lining'? (Actually, why do we?) And why can a drum intro become one of the most recognised drum fills of all time, so much so that it becomes the principle feature in an advert for chocolate?

The point is, so many things please us in a fundamental way that we don't really understand. So why not explain it scientifically?

However you look at it, the Golden Ratio sounds like a pretty impressive piece of kit. In fact, David Bowie went to great lengths to make use of it.

Madness drummer Woody tells me that Bowie had listened to the drum part on the Madness hit 'My Girl' and realised it was exactly the kind of rhythmic approach he wanted for 'Ashes to Ashes'. He spent ages trying out drummers in the US but, although they had no trouble playing the actual part, they weren't able to play it with the right feel. As it turned out, the drummer on *Scary Monsters*, Dennis Davis, played the part with the same feel that Woody had created on 'My Girl'. Thus, finally, the drum part of 'My Girl' was successfully used on 'Ashes to Ashes'.

If you listen to 'Ashes to Ashes', and indeed 'My Girl', the drum patterns in the verses, choruses and middle eights combine to create a perfect sequence of time signatures which are aesthetically very satisfying. Moreover, if you were to dissect the drum parts and calculate the ratios of the different signatures as they appear in the song as a whole, you'd probably find they are equal to The Golden Ratio. In other words, they've both got a great beat, mate.

But what Woody doesn't understand is, why didn't David Bowie just ask him to play on the track in the first place? Presumably it would have saved too much time... and where's the adventure in that?

All this technical stuff can get a bit much, though. That's why we drummers don't usually go on about the cross-pollination of scientific theorems and a musical instrument that is based on entirely natural and deeply soulful instincts. It could get a bit nerdy. But there are exceptions, as Andy Burrows' wife, Steph, found out one night.

Andy had invited two drummer friends round for dinner: Dominic Howard from Muse and Ronnie Vannucci from The Killers. Steph spent much time in happy anticipation as she prepared a nice meal for the three famous drummers assembled in the dining room. After all, it's not every day you get three rock heroes from Razorlight, Muse and The Killers at the same table for dinner. It was guaranteed to be a fairly entertaining evening.

The conversation went something like this:

'I like a bright tone with plenty of sustain, so I generally go for a single ply head on the snare...'

'Yeah, I know what you mean, but I usually fit a double ply on my touring snares for that deep, fat sound...'

'I tell you what, the new DW 9000 Series bass drum pedal really whacks...'

'I like my crash cymbals set fairly level, pretty much perpendicular to the floor...'

'I've discovered I can get a much better feel on the ride if it's not set up too tilted, I'd say an angle of 25 degrees max...'

By nine o'clock Steph had gone to bed.

SECTION 10

SEX, DRUGS AND ROCK'N'ROLL

Drummers Always Get Their Fair Share...

No book containing stories about famous drummers, or indeed any breed of musician, would be complete without a section dedicated to the consumption or ingestion of illegal substances. We've already seen how Topper Headon of The Clash fought and won a battle with drugs. However, on a lighter note...

THE HEALING PROPERTIES OF BURDOCK

Steve 'Vom' Ritchie is the drummer with Die Toten Hosen, a German punk band from Düsseldorf with mass appeal not only in Germany but also South America, Australia and Eastern Europe. The band's name literally means 'The Dead Trousers', but the German phrase 'Tote Hose' is an expression meaning impotent or lifeless. Musically, that couldn't be further from the truth. The band's live shows are a powerhouse of brutal, high energy punk rock, made all the more potent by Vom's playing.

Before moving to Germany in 1990 (he joined Die Toten

Hosen in 1999), Billericay-born Vom was with the English band Dr & The Medics. This story takes us back to 1996, when Vom was back over in England playing in a band called B Bang Cider.

During a break from gigs, Vom agreed to help out on a charity album. It involves a day's recording to lay down seven drum tracks for a charity album called *Sex, Drugs 'N' HIV* to raise awareness and money for AIDS charities. (The HIV project is run by Mat Sargent, former bass player with Sham 69 and the punk band Chelsea.) Around 250 name musicians, including many from the punk era, have agreed to perform on the album free. Most of the material is fast, loud and punky, but also features other musical genres like reggae and New Age.

Vom is the first of seven drummers to each record a track at Sex Pistols' sound engineer and producer Dave Goodman's home studio in Gypsy Hill, South London. He is, after all, known to be 'the Phil Spector of punk' and as such his approach is guaranteed to have a bit of an edge. He is also known for his belief in the power of alternative medicine and crop circles.

Mat is playing guitar as a guide for Vom while he plays the drums on his designated track. Unfortunately, as so often happens on these occasions, something breaks at the start of the session. In this case it's the snare drum skin. While someone is despatched to the nearest music shop to get a replacement, Mat and Vom nip off to the café over the road for a coffee and a fry-up. On their return, they find Dave Goodman in the kitchen of the studio. He has rolled a large cigarette. He looks at Mat and Vom with an air of confidentiality.

'Tell you what, gentlemen, this stuff is amazing.'

'Yeah?'

'It's called burdock. Got it from the health food shop.'

'What does it do then?'

'Not only is it a highly effective tobacco substitute, it actually helps to heal the lungs!'

'Really?'

'Nicotine is an evil weed and people have been using this for thousands of years to clear out lungs. Here, try some.'

Dave passes the cigarette to Mat, who takes a deep draw. And another. Mat nods slowly in recognition of something special and passes it to Vom.

'Try some burdock, Vom?'

'Well, I'm not really a smoker...'

'It has psycho-active properties,' Dave urges him.

'... but I've got a bit of a cough so it might help to clear it!'

Vom takes a drag. He smiles, surprised.

'Hey, I think I can feel the cleansing effect working already...'

Vom takes a few more drags and passes it back to Dave, who continues to look at Vom as if observing the progress of an interesting experiment.

Vom turns his attention to the list of bands and musicians due to perform on the charity album. Something grabs him about one of the entries.

'Who's The Wally Pistols?'

Dave: 'Oh Wally, he's the original Sex Pistols guitarist. He taught Steve [Jones] how to play.'

Vom starts to giggle.

'I thought it was a band turning up called The Wally Pistols.'

Vom quickly descends into a gibbering, giggling wreck as he surveys the rest of the list.

'And who's this, Straplock?'

'Glen Matlock. Straplock's his nick name from the Eater days...'

'And what about Therapy? Are they turning up then or did you just write that for a joke?'

Soon the snare is fixed and it's time to go back into the studio, where Vom is required to play the drums. Dave follows Mat and Vom down into the studio, wearing an elaborate patchwork jacket of many colours. Vom takes one look at this and bursts out laughing.

'So you're wearing your rainbow smiley jacket then... Are you wearing it to get us all off on a trip early before we've even started?'

Dave is humouring him now: 'Yeah, you don't need drugs with a jacket like this...'

'Just cut a tab off and you're away!' Which Vom clearly is.

Vom then appears to be fascinated by the swivel chair which is to act as a makeshift drum stool. He swivels on it like a child.

'Mmm, nice swivel chair – it's the first time I've ever worked with one of these.'

Then there's a problem with Vom's shoe lace, which has got tangled up in the legs of the chair. He bends down to untangle it, which takes him some considerable time. Eventually he manages to get it free and emerges from under the drum kit giggling: 'I thought my shoe lace was a microphone lead. I was trying to get it untangled'

Mat plays a few power chords on his guitar and asks: 'Is that too loud for you?'

Vom doesn't seem to understand. 'Eh? What do you mean, too loud? Oh, I see...' There is much laughter as Vom realises he hasn't yet put his headphones on.

Mat, however, is wearing his headphones, which are held together on one side by gaffer tape wrapped around an old drumstick. This is another source of amusement for Vom. 'I thought you were wearing a radio one... a head set!'

Mat then plays the guitar riff that is the main intro part of the song. He plays the sequence over and over, waiting for Vom to join in on drums. But nothing happens. He looks up at Vom who is staring straight at him: 'Oh, sorry – am I supposed to be playing along as well?'

'That's kind of the idea, Vom... Just come in when you want.'

'It's a good job you looked up or I'd have been sitting here for another half an hour!'

Mat composes himself after another fit of the giggles and begins the intro riff again. After a couple of times round the riff Vom suddenly bursts into life and bashes his floor tom followed by a hard crash on a cymbal. Mat stops playing and is in hysterics as Vom shouts: 'Dinner is served!'

Eventually, Vom gets it together and they get the drum track down successfully. As Mat and Vom roll into the control room to listen to the playback, Dave Goodman says to Vom: 'Well, we got there in the end.'

Vom simply replies: 'Yeah... what's that stuff called again?'

'I call it burdock, but its technical name is cannabis sativa.'

'Eh?'

'Neat grass.'

ALL IN THE CALL OF DUTY

Simon Phillips, son of the well-known bandleader Sid
Phillips, started playing at the age of six. After being
principal drummer in the popular West End show *Jesus
Christ Superstar*, he went on to tour with The Who and
became one of the world's most sought-after session
drummers. He has been Toto's drummer for the past 13 years.

I first met Simon when he was 13 and I was 11, at his
house in Bushey, Hertfordshire, near where I lived. He gave
me my only ever drum lesson on a real drum set, before I
went back home to my boxes and upturned washing-up
bowls. I haven't met him since, but 30-something years later
I contacted him through a mutual drummer friend, John
Lingwood, and he sent me this story about his days playing
the university circuit.

The year is 1975. The band is Chopyn, a recently signed band
on Don Arden's Jet Records. The tour is, well, another one
driving up and down the M1 to various universities around the
United Kingdom. This one happens to be Sheffield University.

I'm sharing a small basement flat in Kensington with our
bass player, Klyde McMullin III. It's the last stop on the pick-
up route. When the van arrives I let the rest of the band and
driver in while, apologetically, I get in the bath. Still, there's
no loading to do, just my cymbal case which is by the front
door as I've been using them for session work in London
between gigs.

Soon we are on our merry way. As luck would have it, we enjoy a traffic and trouble-free trip. The driver, Stuart, has remembered to fill up with gas using some float he's been given by our usually tight-fisted management, so we're spared the usual whip around for petrol money.

As we pull up to the venue I can see down onto the stage through some large windows from the car park, and there's my drum kit, all set up. There's one problem, my lovely tall cymbal stands have nothing on them. How nice, I think, Jeff is cleaning my cymbals.

But curiously, Jeff is standing outside the van! As I step out, he walks towards me with an outstretched hand and his mouth is making the shape and sound of the word 'C Y M B A L S ?'

Oh f***... The penny drops and I realise that they are still sitting in my little basement flat a couple of hundred miles away. That means I'm missing a pair of hi-hats, three crash cymbals, a ride cymbal and a swish cymbal – all Avedis Zildjian.

We've all been there. The problem with being a drummer is there's such a lot of luggage to lug about. And it's expensive stuff, so you can't just pop round the corner and buy replacements for whatever might be missing. We ask the local promoter whether there were any drummers at the university that might lend me some cymbals for the night.

He looks doubtful but after a few enquiries comes back with a couple of names. But apparently it's not good enough simply to ring them up: Jeff and I will have to actually visit these people in their flats, which are scattered around the city. I'm a bit nervous about this. Who is going to lend their prized Zildjian or Paiste cymbals to an 18-year-old kid they've never even met? Still, I've got no choice but to set off on what could be a wild goose chase.

Well, it certainly turns out to be wild. Upon entering the first house Jeff and I are greeted with some degree of suspicion. So, as a kind of initial gesture to secure relations, I am handed a rather large joint.

'You guys been playing long?'

'Yeah, we've been touring for a few months.'

'What's it like? Got any good stories?'

'Well...'

It soon becomes clear that borrowing a student's cymbals entails more than a quick exchange of pleasantries. What follows is almost like some sort of Indian peace pipe meeting where you have to sit on the floor in a circle, smoke and get high together. After a while the students satisfy themselves that we are kosher and I am really the drummer in the band tonight at the university. We manage to borrow a pair of hi-hats and a ride cymbal. The crash cymbals aren't up to much, almost unplayable, so it's off to the next place.

A similar routine ensues. Another sitting circle, another joint or three, and more stories, more convincing. I'm beginning to find this whole business quite amusing. Eventually, although there is still an element of suspicion in the air, we manage to come away with one crash cymbal.

As we walk out into daylight carrying the borrowed cymbals I am startled by the stark reality of fresh air and open streets. Everything seems hazy and almost unreal.

By the time Jeff and I return to the venue we are completely wasted. He puts up the cymbals, which by now consist of a ride, a crash and a pair of hi-hats. But for some reason best known to himself, on the other cymbal stands he sticks these gaudy pink indoor Frisbees made of styrofoam – probably the result of an over-flamboyant sense of ingenuity created by his state of mind at the time. Still, they look good. I'll just have to avoid hitting them.

As show time approaches, I drink endless cups of coffee in a vain attempt to get straight and in a fit state to play. I'm panicking. After all, we may have solved the cymbal problem, but I am now stoned out of my box. And that can be quite unnerving when you're about to go on stage in front of several hundred university students.

As it turns out, I needn't have worried. Even though it's a challenge to play the set as everything seems different – and I can't rely on that auto pilot thing you get when playing a show over and over again – it turns out to be one of our best shows. And not only that, I can hear so much more without all those cymbals crashing away all the time. I learn an enormous amount and I decide to change the way I play the set in future. The whole gig has taught me about the importance of not 'overplaying'. And not to forget my cymbals.

Good for Simon. Even under the heavy influence of marijuana (a condition arrived at in the course of duty), he manages to pull it off and learn something new at the same time. Interesting, though, that someone should consider it perfectly reasonable to confuse the stoned drummer by erecting brightly coloured pretend cymbals among the real ones. Still, his roadie was out of it as well. And anyway, you can always rely on a drummer to rise to the challenge, however bizarre the circumstances.

Drummers usually have a pretty good sense of responsibility when it comes to actually playing the drums, simply because the instrument requires such a high degree of physical co-ordination. We simply cannot deprive ourselves of the use of our limbs and then expect to play a gig or make a record. That's why most of us know our limits and save the over-indulgence for after the performance. It's only when we are asked to perform unexpectedly that disaster can occur...

PAICING IT

I like a drink. Especially when I'm in a pub with lots of friends having a laugh. However, when I'm about to play the drums I naturally watch my consumption. Only once did I ever attempt to play the drums while drunk, and luckily that was round at a mate's house late at night, not at a gig. But I did learn that it can't be done. Not by me, anyway.

Sometimes I find myself asked to play a guest spot at someone else's gig and, if that's a possibility, I exercise a certain amount of restraint just in case. Then there are occasions when I know I won't be playing and can indulge a little more freely.

John Lingwood found himself in exactly that situation back in the early '90s. It was at a memorial to celebrate the life of Tony Ashton, of '60s band Ashton, Gardner And Dyke fame, and the gig featured several well-known drummers. At the end of the proceedings, a grand finale was scheduled, during which all the drummers were to perform together.

This would incorporate some seriously clever rudiments and flashy interactions between some notorious stars: Zak Starkey, Henry Spinetti and Ian Paice. Quite a drumming line-up.

John, although not scheduled to play that day, had been invited to attend the event and avail himself of the entertainment and, of course, the food and drink that was there in abundance. Like everybody else gathered there, he ate and drank heartily, safe in the knowledge that nothing else was expected of him. Then, as the hour of the grand finale approached, he was tapped on the shoulder. He turned round to find Zak Starkey looking furtive.

John: 'You OK, Zak? You look in a hurry!'

Zak: 'Yeah! Listen mate, I'm gonna shoot off now – got something else I've gotta do. You don't mind filling in, do you?'

Before John could reply, someone tapped him on the other shoulder and handed him another glass of fine red wine. When he turned back round, Zak had disappeared.

Moments later, he looked up at the stage to see Henry seated at his drums, Ian at his and an empty space where Zak should have been. Ordinarily, he would have been eager to join in. But he knew he'd had too many – far too many. And red wine and drumming don't really mix. Some lager maybe, but not red wine. He decided to make his escape there and then but suddenly, as if it had been planned, Neil Murray (guitarist with such legends as Whitesnake and Black Sabbath) pointed to him and beckoned him up to the stage.

There are times when being asked to do something you're good at when you feel you can't – or simply don't want to –

can result in one of two outcomes. Either you do it and sod the consequences, or you refuse and look like a prima donna. John figured that it was a fair cop and the former approach was the right way to go. Feeling pissed but inclined to make the best of the situation, John sat down behind the unmanned kit and hit the snare a couple of times in a slightly haphazard way. Ian Paice responded to this with a cheeky gesture in the form of his famous one-handed roll. The challenge had been set.

As it happened, the number to be performed was 'Resurrection Shuffle' – Ashton, Gardner and Dyke's big hit from 1970. This involved some serious snare drum shuffle work, interspersed with various fills and cross-rhythms to spark up the drum trio spectacle. As it turned out, it all went very well. John recalls being told by people in the audience how impressive it sounded. Of course he was delighted with that verdict, but had a private verdict of his own: 'Not from where I was sitting...' On this occasion he felt the song should have been retitled 'Resuscitation Shuffle'.

A drummer certainly has to be careful not to be taken unawares. In 1986 I was recording an album with a band called The Johnnies. We were doing an all-night session in a 24-track studio that was part of a university specialising in performance arts. The facility had been provided by the resident studio engineer, Soron, who happened to like the band's material (copyright Paul Jensen).

Soron was an excellent engineer and loved music with a passion. He was equally passionate about smoking marijuana. In those days I was fairly partial, too. However, during the session I declined every time a joint was passed my way.

After some hours we finally finished all the backing tracks to the album. No more drumming for me, so next time a joint was passed around I felt able to indulge myself, which I did, gratefully. However, on taking a few drags and passing it on, I was little prepared for the severity of the effect it would have on me. This was really strong stuff. Lucky I'd finished my bit. Then Soron made an announcement…

'I'm really sorry guys, but I've accidentally wiped that last track. We'll have to go for another take!'

And so I ended up back behind my kit, stoned out of my box. The drums seemed strangely weird, not the same as I had perceived them earlier. I was wondering how I could negotiate the operation of this instrument to an acceptable degree when I looked up to see our keyboard player, Phil, in the control room, looking through the studio window. For some inexplicable reason, I was convinced he was absolutely furious with me. I don't just mean a bit cross, but seething with rage.

How could I have been so outrageously badly behaved? The whole session's been ruined by my cocky, druggy self.

Of course, Phil wasn't in the slightest bit annoyed. In fact, he hadn't got a clue I'd even smoked anything. It was simply my overworked imagination fuelled by ever-increasing paranoia brought on by the blow.

We went for a couple of new takes and it felt like someone else was playing. I had absolutely no clue what I was doing.

It wasn't helped by the fact that this song was a particularly up-tempo rocker with loads of stops and starts at the end of the verses and choruses.

We managed to get it right in a couple of takes, although there is a brief hesitation after one of the aforementioned stops, evidence of my condition. As it turned out, everyone was stoned and wouldn't have noticed anyway. And considering the state Soron must have been in, we were lucky he hadn't wiped the whole album.

Cannabis, marijuana, skunk – call it what you like, it simply doesn't go with playing the drums to order on a recording or at a gig. Woody from Madness remembers (just) playing stoned on one occasion...

WOODY'S NIGHTMARE

We're about to go on stage supporting The Dead Kennedys at a club in San Francisco. Someone passes me a tiny, single-skin roll-up containing a bit of blow. I'm thinking, 'Well it's only a tiny little rolly – surely one drag won't hurt? Yeah, what the hell...'

Next thing I know I'm sitting behind what I assume is my drum kit wondering where the hell I am. Somehow I've got to play an entire Madness set in front of a couple of thousand people.

I really don't know how, but my autopilot kicks in and I find myself playing the drums reasonably well. My mind wanders a bit and I'm having to concentrate on keeping myself in check and it's not easy, but it looks as though I'm going to wing it. But at one point it gets really scary. We're into 'My Girl' and my mind wanders a bit too far. Suddenly I wake up from my reverie to discover I've no idea how far we are into the song.

We seem to have been playing this song for ages. We must be near the end surely! So I begin to go into what I think should be the ending. I start crashing the cymbals, one after the other, which is what happens towards the final stop. However, at the very last moment, something stops me from stopping. I've no idea how, but somewhere deep at the back of my mind, a rational voice quietly informs me that we have only just come out of the piano solo that's featured in the middle of the song.

I pull myself together and go back into the song. Phew...

Ever since then I've never smoked anything before playing the drums, it's just not worth all the problems it can cause. In fact, I don't bother with drugs or alcohol at all these days.

Not much choice for Woody but to carry on there really. He could hardly get up to leave saying, 'Sorry everyone, I am ridiculously stoned – we'll just have to skip tonight...' Perhaps he could have pretended to collapse with back pain, but, as we've seen, drummers generally tend to carry on under any kind of duress. His muscle memory must have been working overtime that night – all that cymbal crashing after the piano solo would have sounded totally wrong. Lucky he realised just in time: imagine if he had stopped altogether!

SHOCK AFTER AFTERSHOCK

Another story from Russell Gilbrook of Uriah Heep, about something that happened at the Download metal festival in

2004, featuring Metallica supported by Slipknot and Slayer. Russell was playing with a band called Planet Of Women on a smaller stage in a nearby marquee.

We've just finished playing on one of the smaller stages in this side tent to about a thousand people. The gig's gone well and I'm looking forward to watching Metallica on the main stage.

As I've finished my playing for the day I'm in the mood to party, so I pop backstage to get a drink. Holding a pint of Red Aftershock in one hand and a pint of Green Aftershock in the other, I get chatting to a mate who is tec'ing for one of the local bands. Soon he has to rush off, so I go out to watch Slipknot.

After working up a thirst crowd-surfing, I'm backstage again after their set. There seems to be a bit of a commotion with people from Metallica's crew making frantic phone calls. I figure it's probably some technical hitch they'll fix pretty quickly – after all, this is Metallica – so I rush out to catch the beginning of their set. The crowd are pretty fired up and I'm pretty pissed – just the right circumstances to enjoy a good blast of metal from the experts.

The problem is, nothing seems to be happening.

We wait...

We wait...

And we wait.

Eventually, after two hours, the band comes on. But without their regular drummer. The man behind the kit is Joey Jordison from Slipknot. Later on in the set he's replaced by Dave Lombardo from Slayer. I soon realise, in my heady state, that Metallica's drummer must have fallen ill at the last minute.

The next morning I wake up feeling pretty rough. I switch my phone on to see if I've received any messages. I've got three, all from the guy I was chatting to backstage after my gig. As I play them back, I kick myself.

'Russell, Metallica's drummer, has had an accident and can't play. They're desperate for a drummer. They've got the guys from the supports to do some numbers but they need another!'

'Russ, it's me again! Where are you? If you get this message get yourself backstage sharpish. Metallica are rehearsing with Slipknot and Slayer's drummers but they can't learn it all in an hour or so. We need you to do a couple of numbers to ease the pressure.'

So all the time I was standing in the crowd waiting for Metallica to come on, they were rehearsing the two other drummers *and* looking for me! Mind you, I was so out of it by that time I couldn't have played anyway.

The somewhat bohemian lifestyle associated with rock drummers, and indeed pop musicians as a whole, is well documented. Mums usually worry when their offspring express a genuine desire to propel themselves into the world of pop music, especially when they are quite young...

SEX, DRUGS AND ROCK 'N' ROLL

Here's another tale from Steve White about his early days as a drummer. Even when Steve reached his late teens his mum still had her concerns, in particular all that stuff you hear about pop stars and what they get up to....

The year is 1983. I am a 17-year-old drummer who started playing drums when my mum and dad bought my first drum set at the age of nine. Since then all I've ever really wanted to do is play the drums. In fact, when I was a boy I insisted on taking a pair of sticks wherever I went. My mum used to worry a bit, but since I started getting into bands a few years ago she's been more relaxed about my passion for the drums.

Then one day my dream comes true. I get the job with Paul Weller who wants me to be the drummer in his new band, The Style Council. Wow! What an opportunity for a 17-year-old! Apparently it's a month of rehearsals and then we're off on tour, first stop Hamburg! I tell my mum and dad who are thrilled for me: 'We always knew you had it in you, well done!' Even though she's pleased for me, I can tell by the look on my mum's face that she's worried about it.

So a month later my parents drive me to the car park in North London where the tour bus is waiting. We say our goodbyes and they walk with me as I carry my bags to the coach. Standing beside the coach door is a rather large chap. He is built like an ox, has a big black beard and seems to block the doorway entirely. He introduces himself as Kenny Wheeler, then turns to my mum and says: 'Mrs White, I know it must have been on your mind, the sex and the drugs and the rock 'n' roll...'

'Well, yes...'

'No need to worry. It's my job to make sure he gets his fair share of all of 'em.'

SECTION 11

NATURE'S CALL

When A Drummer Has To Go, He Has To Go...

Every musician knows what it's like to be on stage and need the toilet. For drummers, however, it's a little more of an issue. For a start, if you need to go to the toilet but can't, flailing your limbs around in all directions tends to make the situation worse. Moreover, it's often more difficult for a drummer to just up sticks and bugger off. Of course we do our best to make sure that all that kind of business is taken care of beforehand, but it doesn't always go according to plan.

FEAR AND LOATHING IN BELFAST DOCKS

Chris Hickey was drummer with punk band The Perfect Crime, which featured singer Paul Lerwell, who used to be in Rosetta Stone. He is currently drummer with covers band The Branstons. I caught up with Chris in the Horns pub venue in Watford, where he told me about a particularly unpleasant business back in 1980.

He was playing a gig in Belfast with The Perfect Crime.

Although it was 1980, the punk scene was still as lively and voracious in Belfast as it had been in London in the mid-'70s. The problem with drumming is that it involves such a great deal of acrobatics and jerky movements, especially around the buttock and groin area, the pivotal point from which we operate our foot pedals. So Chris can't exactly sit still and hang in there, so to speak. And of course, this is punk, not backroom jazz.

I am sitting behind my drum kit on a smallish stage in a notoriously rough pub called The Harp Bar on Belfast Docks. It's full of vicious punks and skinheads looking forward to a night of random barbarism. We begin our set and immediately the usual combination of jumping, spitting and pogoing ensues. This evening's mayhem seems to be in particular earnest and we are sprayed with saliva and congealed mucus significantly more heavily than usual. Not only that, we are also bombarded by items whose potential for harm varies from a simple apple to a broken bottle. Added to this, there is one particular character near the front of the stage who has apparently singled me out for special attention and is mouthing expletives at me with an expression of such insane hatred that there can be little doubt as to his fondness for random murder.

Then there is the fact that I had a large, hot curry last night with many beers. My body's digestive system chooses this moment to complete its operation with some considerable enthusiasm. The angry punk in the front is not giving up and neither are my bowels, over which my control is rapidly diminishing. The only hope is for me to hold out until the interval.

Uriah Heep's Russell Gilbrook.   © Courtesy of Russell Gilbrook

Above: Dan Woodgate, better known as Woody, the drummer
with Madness. © *Andrew Aitchison*

Below: Mike Wade found fame as part of The New Seekers.

Above: Duallist drums played by Saxon's Nigel Glocker.   © *Kevin Mackie*

Below: After Mohair split in 2009, Pete Baker has continued to play with a variety of bands.

ove: Status Quo's Matt Letley.

low: Pink Floyd's Nick Mason.

© *Paddy Brownlee*

© *Jill Furmanovsky*

Above: Steve 'Jock' Birnie, drummer and inmate of Ford open prison.

Below: Since Steve White played with the Style Council his career has included a USA tour with Oasis. *© James Cumpsty*

Simon Phillips a veteran drummer who plays with Toto.

Session drummer Tim Goldsmith.

The Clash's Topper Headon.
© *Pennie Smith*

The inevitable happens and I crap myself with such ferocity that playing punk drums is rendered an unbelievably uncomfortable business. Not only is sitting still completely out of the question, the aforementioned vigour required from my movements has a kind of 'spreading and pasting' effect. It is almost as though I am turning the whole thing into some kind of involuntary celebration of the bowel movement process.

However, if such a thing is possible, I am distracted by another spectacle. A punk is leaning over a stairwell which overlooks the stage and vomiting over the keyboard player with an impassioned zest which, had I not been in such discomfort myself, might have put me in mind of a classic gothic gargoyle come to life.

The first set ends with my band mates covered in mucus and sick, and I am sitting in shit. Well, at least it's my own. I take the opportunity to rush to the toilets where, of course, I am reminded that the sanitary facilities at these establishments are sadly inadequate even for people who need to undergo only the slightest of ablutions, let alone the kind of repair work that I have in mind. No door, no running water and best of all, no toilet paper. I will spare you any further details of my nightmare but it's as well that in those days nice big boxer shorts had not yet been invented.

Chris told me that the rest of the gig remained as barbaric, although he felt a little more comfortable having discarded his underpants into Belfast Docks via a toilet window. The frenzied punk at the front continued to mouth obscenities and threats of death, and when it was over and the band was packing up,

Chris found a dart stuck through his bass drum skin. Nervous at having had a lucky escape, he turned round to see the punk approaching him, looking wild-eyed with intent. However, he simply smiled and said quite politely: 'Great gig mate, thanks! Nice one!' Unfortunately, the relief came too late and Chris had to revisit the toilet with a bar towel.

ENCORE

Gary Powell, formerly with The Libertines and current drummer with The Dirty Pretty Things, told me this story about an embarrassing incident a few years ago.

Boston, Massachusetts. You are in the front row of a huge auditorium watching one of your favourite bands, The Dirty Pretty Things, come to the end of their set. It's been one helluva good show. Plenty of on-stage acrobatics with relentless helpings of sharp, high energy showstoppers one after the other. Just how you like it. As you focus on the drummer, Gary Powell, giving it everything he's got with a look of real determined passion on his face, it seems unimaginable that anything could be wrong.

But far from being evidence of impassioned involvement, Gary's facial contortions are the product of something rather more basic. He needs a dump real bad. The kind of feeling you get when you've eaten something dodgy or contracted a bug. Of course, under normal circumstances this is easily dealt with, but not when you're on stage in front of several thousand people at the height of a gig.

So Gary's priorities have changed dramatically. He needs a lavatory – fast. As soon as his final cymbal crash has been delivered, he's off. The rest of the band are waving at the crowd as they leave the stage to wait a couple of minutes before returning for their well deserved encore, unaware that Gary is running for England down the backstage corridor. Unfortunately, when he finally bursts into the loo, he discovers to his horror that all the cubicles are locked with 'out of order' slapped on them.

This is bad news indeed. Not only that, the tour manager is at the other end of the corridor calling him back for the encore.

So Gary gets back behind his kit and makes the best of it. He's simply got to hold out to the end. As Chris Hickey will tell you, playing the drums with your pants full of shit is not a comfortable business. Gary does well. He holds it all together, so to speak. But at the end of the encore, the crowd want more. This is just too much. He signifies to the rest of the band as best he can by mouthing 'No more' and runs for it.

As he darts down the backstage corridor once more, he knows there's only one solution: the ladies. So he throws what little caution he has left to the wind, runs into the ladies toilets and in a blind panic selects the first cubicle. He gets his pants down just in time and lets rip with all the gratifying force of a desperate man on the cusp of blessed relief. Made it!

As the dust settles, he congratulates himself, as men do, on the seemingly unique and impressive pungency of his excretion. He also makes a mental note to get out of the ladies as quickly as possible, as he'd really rather not share this achievement with a member of the opposite sex. Probably best to go and wash his hands in the gents next door.

Gary finishes his business and opens the cubicle, only to discover a couple of ladies using the mirror to administer lipstick at the other end of the toilets. They must have heard the whole thing. And the smell! He attempts a quick exit. Just as he thinks he's got away with it, one of them says: 'Nice show!'

And the other: 'What do you do for an encore?'

So next time you see a drummer's face distorted with passion, remember: things aren't necessarily what they seem.

TAKING THE PISS

Imagine. You are a German lover of British pop music from the '60s and '70s. You are a particular fan of Manfred Mann's Earth Band, so much so that not only do you have all the singles from 'Do Wah Diddy' and 'The Mighty Quinn' to 'Blinded by the Light', but you also have a passion for the more obscure tracks, your favourite of which is 'Redemption Song'. This is a progressive piece, which has a quiet, melodic refrain in the middle featuring a lovely guitar solo accompanied by lush, atmospheric keyboards from Manfred himself.

It is this particular part of the set that you are looking forward to as you travel to see your favourite band of all time not far from your hometown, Düsseldorf. You eagerly anticipate the excitement of a live performance because you know that the music will sound extra special, as the band use creative variation in their performances to give that little bit more to the audience's enjoyment of the music; the fundamental ingredient to every live show.

Sure enough, the band do not disappoint. In fact, you are

even more overwhelmed by the performance of Manfred's set than you had so far anticipated. As 'Redemption Song' begins, you look forward to that melodic refrain in the middle with real eagerness. After all, it's the highlight of the set for you.

But when the moment arrives, the aforementioned guitar section is completely devoid of the lush keyboard accompaniment that creates the mood you love so much. You look to the stage to see why Manfred is not playing to discover that he is not there. Nor, for that matter, is the drummer, John Lingwood.

As the guitarist finishes the piece, Manfred leaps out of the wings onto the stage to finish the song while John Lingwood reappears behind his kit. Of course, you've no idea why these two went missing during what should have been your favourite bit of the show. You figure you'll probably never know, but you assume it must have been an unfortunate technical problem of some kind. Ah well, can't be helped. That's life!

Rewind to the same time, same place. You are a fly on the wall underneath the stage at the front of the huge auditorium. Manfred Man and John Lingwood are standing side by side, urinating into a large dustbin. A lone guitar solo is being played on the stage above. John turns to Manfred and says: 'Aren't you supposed to be playing on this bit, Manfred?'

As the man in the audience, if you'd been told the real reason why your favourite moment in the set had failed to materialise, you would probably put it down to one of rock 'n' roll's more peculiar extravagances. And hey, there's nothing like a little creative variation.

MAD, BAD AND DANGEROUS

GINGER TAKES THE PISS

Ginger Baker is perhaps best known for his work with Eric Clapton and Jack Bruce in '60s band Cream. He went on to form Blind Faith with Clapton and Stevie Winwood, after which he created Ginger Baker's Air Force. Following that he teamed up with Paul and Adrian Gurvitz to form the Baker Gurvitz Army. I have not actually had the privilege of meeting Ginger, but a friend of mine remembers seeing him in concert many years ago.

It was in the days when audiences generally remained seated, expressing their appreciation of the music by moving their heads. At the beginning of a concert, a few would begin to nod in time to the music. As the evening progressed, variations would begin, incorporating side-to-side movements into the up and down motion. As the audience collectively gained more confidence and their involvement in the music intensified, the movements would become more erratic and the auditorium would resemble a sea of hair flying in all directions. In the latter part of the concert, people would continue the process standing up, some daring to move into the isles while the supervisors turned a blind eye. This later became known as 'head banging'.

A friend of mine was at one such event: a concert featuring Ginger Baker on drums, way back in 1972. It was at the stage when the hair was starting to fly and people were beginning to get up from their seats. After one particular song, which had met with frantic and rapturous applause, everything came to a complete halt as Ginger Baker came out from behind his drum kit, strolled to the front of the stage and addressed the audience over the singer's microphone: 'I'm just going for a piss!'

He then left the stage to use the toilet. However, instead of filling in with some improvised jamming or verbal banter, the rest of the band stood in complete silence until he returned about five minutes later. Now, that might not seem very long, but if you've just spent an hour or so building up to a frenzied head bang and left your seat in anticipation of some kind of euphoric climax to the concert, it might just take the wind out of your sails, or hair even. However, this occurred during an age when it was cool to be laid back about virtually everything.

And, of course, it gave everyone a chance to skin up.

SECTION 12

TECHNICAL HITCH

Drummers Don't Start Out
As Technicians...

When drumming was invented, man hadn't had much truck with electricity. His communication skills were limited to banging drums, making fires for smoke signals and grunting. Thunderstorms scared the pants off him and the last thing on his mind was to try and understand them. In a sense, thousands of years later, the physical act of creating and sustaining rhythm is still essentially a primeval one, worlds apart from the complexities of studio technology.

But as these technologies become more complex, drummers are increasingly moving with the times, and many established drummers have great skills when it comes to operating today's complex digital recording facilities. Indeed, many of them, like Gavin Harrison (of Renaissance, Porcupine Tree and lately King Crimson), have these in-house and are thus able to operate as session players from home, playing the tracks to a specified brief and sending the finished product down the line to the artist.

But when drum machines and click tracks were first invented, we drummers had to learn a whole new way of approaching life in the studio...

WELCOME TO THE MACHINE

Pink Floyd drummer Nick Mason was there when the band formed at the Regent Street Polytechnic back in 1964, pioneering early stage lighting effects that led to psychedelic pop and the elaborate shows that we are used to today. He was the man behind the kit on all of Floyd's recordings, including the 1973 masterpiece *Dark Side of the Moon*. He's still playing drums, at rare Floyd reunions and on occasions with Roger Waters and David Gilmour on their solo shows, as well as various ongoing projects. Nick has also produced for Steve Hillage, Robert Wyatt, The Damned and Gong amongst others. He also has a great sense of humour.

The scene is Mayfair Studios, Primrose Hill, North London in 1982, and Pink Floyd are working on their album *The Final Cut*. James Guthrie is doing the honours as producer. Not only is he a highly experienced studio engineer, he also has a keen understanding of how to work with the eccentricities and sometimes unpredictable behaviour of the band, both individually and as a whole.

On this occasion, a rhythm groove has been programmed into the recently invented Linn drum machine. Nick Mason arrives to overdub live drums onto the track. It's a new way of doing things which requires a blending of rigid, pre-programmed time signatures with the natural variants inherent in real, live drumming.

Of course, when you try and combine these two methods,

the disciplines required are not always at your fingertips, so to speak. James notices, with some trepidation, that such is the case today. After all, even if you have got loads of experience dealing with Pink Floyd in the studio, how do you tell a world-famous drummer in a world-famous band that he's not, on this occasion, getting it right?

James decides to adopt the direct approach. Nick is an intelligent and reasonable guy and can take a little criticism. So he calls Nick into the control room.

'Nick, there's something not quite right here…'

'Oh? What's up?'

'Well, there seem to be some discrepancies…'

(Nick nods)

'…between the drum part we laid down on the drum machine…'

(Nick nods)

'…and what you're doing over the top.'

(Nick nods)

'It's, erm, just that the timing is slightly out…'

(Nick nods)

'…and, well, it's kind of a consistency problem…'

At this point, Nick says: 'You know, James, timing and consistency were never my strong points. I was always much better at the after-gig parties.'

If you need someone to take the sting out of any situation, always ask a drummer.

ROCK BOTTOM SESSION

Nick also recalls a moment when he was producing Robert Wyatt's 1974 album, *Rock Bottom*.

I'm working on a Robert Wyatt album. He and I are co-producing the sessions and today we're privileged to have the superb Laurie Allan in the studio to do the drum parts. He has a lovely light touch to his playing which we know will provide just the right feel for each track.

Laurie is behind his unique miniature kit [he used tiny timpani made by Sonor, originally designed for schools, instead of regular toms] and Robert and I are in the control room, raring to go. We send him the first track for the run through. It's difficult to describe what happens next.

Laurie simply goes berserk. He's playing a completely free-jazz, arrhythmic solo over the whole piece. His playing is totally devoid of even the slightest degree of sensitivity, time-keeping or respect for the music. Robert and I look at each other in horror. As the senior producer I naturally delegate the job of informing Laurie that it's a bit too contemporary for our taste to Robert. So Robert decides that diplomacy is the order of the day and hits the talk-back button...

'Alright, Laurie?'

'Hi, guys. Is there a problem?'

'The thing is, Laurie, it's not really the kind of thing we were after...'

'Sorry?'

'The style is a bit too contemporary for us.'

'But...'

'No offence, modern freestyle jazz is great stuff, and what you're doing fits quite nicely, it's just that these tracks were written with a more traditional vein in mind...'

'Sorry guys, I think we've got our wires crossed here...'

Laurie then explains that he has received nothing in his

headset. He was simply checking the positioning and warming up. Burning with embarrassment, Robert and I apologise to the bemused Laurie, who simply gets on and delivers exactly what we want.

But it's not always the drummers who get all mixed up with the technicalities...

TECHNICAL HITCH

For nearly 10 years Matt Letley has been the drummer with Status Quo. He started playing drums at the age of six and during his career has played with artists like David Essex, Bob Geldof, Kim Wilde, A-ha and the Pet Shop Boys. This story takes us back to the late 1990s, when Matt is booked for a session in a studio just outside Dublin to record an album for the Irish singer, Michael English.

The place is a small budget studio, not really geared up to record real drums on a daily basis. But the owner/engineer is very amiable and keen to please – a true native of the Emerald Isle. He sets to work busily making technical adjustments, rewiring sends and returns, busses and auxiliaries to accommodate the recording of live drums.

Meanwhile, Michael, myself and the rest of the session musicians begin to look through the charts and routine for the first song. Soon we're all ready to go for a take.

I sit behind the kit, now fully mic-ed up, and put on my headphones, as do the rest of the band. We go through the song a couple of times to get a comfortable headphone mix and establish the right tempo. Once everyone's happy, I give a thumbs-up to the engineer, who is now in the control room and ask him to set up a cowbell loop on the studio's drum machine as a click track.

'OK,' comes his voice through my headphones, via the talkback mic. A few moments later, it's thumbs up all round as he says: 'Here comes the click…we're recording.'

As we start playing I realise I can't hear the click. So I stop the take. Apparently the other guys can hear it. So can the engineer in the control room. The only person who can't hear it is me. The engineer opens up the talkback mic: 'Have you got your volume turned up?'

'Yes. I can hear the other instruments, I just can't hear the click!'

The engineer jumps up from his seat and bounds into the studio, looking puzzled. He does some frantic rewiring. He pulls leads out, plugs others in, swaps others over: 'Try that!' Then he hurries back to the control room.

After a little fiddling around, his voice comes into the headphones: 'OK! Here comes the click…'

'Nothing.'

'Have you still not got it?'

'Nope.'

Silence for a while. Then the engineer opens the talkback mic once more and says in his broad Dublin accent: 'Are you sure your headphones are plugged in?'

For drummers, studio experiences can vary from exasperating to plain ludicrous…

SPIKE WEBB

TURN UP THE TALENT

Ed Sylvester has played with pop/rock band The Zeds for about four years in and around London and Watford. Previously he drummed for Southampton band Naked Season. He told me the highlight of the band's career was being played on the Steve Wright Breakfast Show when he was on Radio 1 in the mid-'90s...

In our naivety, we sat on the stairs waiting for the phone to ring. It didn't and we carried on doing pub gigs for the next ten years.

Anyway, the recording session that produced our one and only airplay was done in a local Southampton studio called Sound On Sound. It was basically the cheapest place we could find – essentially a couple of Portakabins stuck together with bits of old conservatories, front doors, and whatever random bits of wood the owner could find. A self-build in every sense of the word. Outside stood a full size model of the Tardis, and inside is a full working model of R2D2.

The drum room was separated from the rest of the studio by double-glazing panels of assorted sizes, and mics hung from the ceiling on old coat hangers. Imagine if the Wombles had built a studio – this was it. Mike, the guy who ran the studio was a Mormon. A 6ft 4in giant with size 14 feet and a dodgy 'tash, he was scary as hell to look at, but the nicest guy you'll ever meet, with that all-important degree of tolerance you need to run a recording studio.

So with this patchwork studio and a self-taught sound engineer, what sort of sound could we possibly hope for from

Sound On Sound? Well, remarkably professional actually, which was why we went back there to record our fifth studio CD later that year. The session went really well and I got my drum tracks down in one day. Well, they don't call me 'One Take Ed' for nothing.

But two weeks later I got a phone call: 'Ed, we're having real problems with the drums you put down.'

'What's the problem? Out of time? Speeding up? Kick drum in the wrong place?'

'Well, yes, all of that – you are a drummer, after all. But there's a new problem.'

'Whassat?'

'Your cymbals are too quiet. Mike says you didn't hit them hard enough.'

'Hmmmm.'

I've seen Ed play several times and he hits the cymbals with all the gusto you need for rocky pop songs. If he didn't hit the cymbals properly, he simply wouldn't be in the band. If cymbals aren't coming across properly on a recording, it is most likely a technical fault. Why would a drummer go into a studio and suddenly start playing like Mary Poppins?

My mantra is: if you didn't tell me something was wrong at the time, I'm not coming back in to do the whole lot again. I have more gear to set up than anyone else and, more importantly, coming back in would be an admission of some kind of fault on my part – and I am 100 per cent sure that whatever this was, it wasn't down to me.

Somehow they found the volume on the cymbals – or more likely Mike turned up the all-important 'talent button' which every studio engineer seems to have hidden away. The track sounded great and, as ever, the rest of the band didn't even notice the real mistakes on the drum parts.

SECTION 13

SOMETHING STUPID

Some Things Can Be A Huge Embarrassment For Drummers...

NICE WORK IF YOU CAN GET IT

Steve Dixon is playing for Ray Davies' band at a festival in Belgium. They are support to headliners Status Quo, along with Squeeze, Cockney Rebel, Ten Years After and The Mike Flowers Pops.

It's a big event and everything is a bit chaotic. Usually I have someone to set my drums up but there's no one around and it's getting near show time, so I set them up myself on a movable riser. Soon it's our turn to play and as I hear a huge crowd calling for Ray Davies, my riser is moved into place. Then it's curtain up and we're on. The gig goes really well and we leave the stage to roaring cheers as the curtain comes back down for the changeover to Quo.

There are still no drum roadies around so I figure I might as well start dismantling my kit. I take down the stool and hi-hat stand, and then move round to the front of the riser to dismantle the rack toms. Suddenly a wave of light engulfs me. I realise the curtain's gone back up and look round to see 10,000 people watching me...

That's the same 10,000 people who saw Steve playing the same kit only a few minutes before. A little embarrassing, to say the least. Steve tells me it was just a slip up. Perhaps the audience thought he was supplementing his income by helping the road crew.

THAT'LL TEACH YOU TO SHOW OFF

Here's another tale featuring Nigel Glockner of Saxon. This one describes a drumming moment that left him a tad embarrassed during his early days with the band.

I'm on my second tour as Saxon's drummer. One of the crowd favourites is the song 'Motorcycle Man' off the *Wheels of Steel* album. Traditionally, Saxon's original drummer, Pete Gill, had put in a fast triplet fill on two rack toms during the song's intro. For some reason (I don't know why), I hadn't put it in on the last tour and up until now have never bothered with it. But one night the guys suggest I include it. After all, it is an exciting intro. I've got a great deal with Ludwig and have recently acquired a kit that includes ten toms, starting at a six-inch concert tom and going through to an 18-inch floor tom.

Still, being a bit of a new boy in the band I'm thinking I've got something to prove, so I'm wondering if I can possibly do the same fill in the same two bars but use every tom – all ten of them! So, at the next sound check I count the band in, here comes the fill and I go for it. Suddenly I realise I'm going so fast I'm losing control. By the time I've reached the big 18-inch drum I literally I can't stop. The momentum keeps me going and I run out of drums to hit.

Next thing I know I'm flying off the back of the drum riser, which is pretty high up. I crash into a heap on the ground below. Then, to maximise my injury, two drum wedge monitors come crashing down on top of me.

When a drummer decides to have an accident, it will usually incorporate a series of elaborate knock-on effects that inevitably draw further attention to his initial folly. And there will be no sympathy.

TOOLS OF THE TRADE

There are some circumstances in which a drummer cannot avoid descending into blind panic – the kind of fumbling mess reminiscent of disastrous gig situations usually associated with bad equipment, bad management and youthful inexperience.

It was summer 2002 in Amersham, Hertfordshire. A charity event in aid of something or other was being held at a football club. A half-moon stage had been erected in the grounds outside the club bar and the whole affair had a family bring-your-babies-and-dogs feel about it, complete with barbeque, a busy bar with infuriatingly slow volunteers dispensing drinks and a general crowd of musicians milling around, waiting to sound check.

The event was to be headlined by Paul Young's Los Pacaminos, supported by two bands, the second being ourselves. We were called Texas Flood and yes, we were a

Stevie Ray Vaughn tribute band, with other stuff thrown in. I was not their regular drummer, but one of several they call upon when their regular guy, who plays with The Glen Millar tribute band, couldn't make it.

Now, these chaps can really play. They have, over the years, studied the Ray Vaughn style as if it was a history degree and I defy anyone to emulate that particular sound any more convincingly. This also means that whoever plays the drums with them has to shape up pretty well, concentrate on the ska-blues swing style while maintaining a rocky edge in the process. For my part, I've never been particularly adept at jazz-style snare shuffles with the left hand, but I've got the hang of it to an acceptable degree and it's always an enjoyable challenge.

Except in this instance.

As ever on these occasions, everything was running late. We had no time for a sound check but that didn't bother us overmuch. What I hadn't bargained for was the lack of an equipment check. A drum kit had been hired for the support bands. As it turned out, the drummer before me had brought his own kit and dismantled it immediately after he'd finished. I then had ten whole minutes to find a kit in time for our 30-minute set. Given that we'd been told there was strictly no run-over potential, any messing about on my part would encroach significantly upon our performance. On asking the young man in charge of the hired equipment where the drums were, he pointed to an area underneath the stage and indicated drum cases and a large stands and fitments box.

On further inspection I discovered that the fittings box

contained a mish-mash of old cymbal stands, a horrible bass drum pedal (the type that fixes onto the drum rim via a flimsy wing nut) and a broken hi-hat clutch. Great. And now I've got seven minutes left. At the most.

In a slightly whimpering voice I asked the young man if this was the full extent of the equipment with regard to drum sets, to which he replied magnanimously: 'Yes! That's right, it's all there, help yourself!'

I mentioned something about the difficulties I was likely to encounter but he simply replied that he didn't know much about drums himself so I'd have to piece it altogether as best I could.

Five minutes left.

I won't go into details of the frantic rummaging and cursing that followed. Suffice to say that I delayed the Texas Flood performance by about five minutes. We started with a mid-paced, straightforward rocker called 'House Is A Rockin'', which went surprisingly well drum-wise.

The audience were warmly enthusiastic and we felt good. We had a good fold-back system and we were on a big stage with lights and everything, probably playing to fellow musicians of some considerable stature in the form of Los Pacaminos. This was going to be fun after all. So we went into 'Let Me Love You Baby', a ska-blues shuffle that required the kind of aforementioned rhythmic subtleties often associated with Stevie Ray Vaughn material.

It was then that the real nightmare began to unfold.

I had discovered during my frantic assembly of the drum kit that the hi-hat clutch wasn't actually broken, but was a new design that featured various hooks and cranes that I didn't understand. I had managed to fix it successfully to the top hat and the centre rod and hoped this would hold out.

Of course, it didn't. In fact, it came completely loose so that the hi-hat was inoperative, rendering my left leg useless. This would have been OK normally: I would ride on the ride cymbal until the end of the song and quickly tighten it up before the next one. But because I didn't understand the leverage systems deployed in the new invention, this turned out not to be possible. Anyway, there was the bass pedal to deal with, which had become all but completely detached from the drum.

On top of this, the bass drum itself had wandered forward, as they will do when there is no drum carpet and you're on a shiny, wooden stage. For the icing on the cake, the snare drum had also wandered, but in reverse. So I had to pull the bass drum back into position, push the snare out of my crotch and re-attach my bass pedal (f*** the hi-hat, that was a gonner), all while Geoff, our guitarist, began the very short intro to the next song. And Paul Young was probably watching too. Shit.

Having made the intro in the nick of time (although I confess I came in on the back beat as opposed to the first beat of the bar, for which I received a side glance), I hoped all would be well. Fat chance. This kit wasn't letting me off that lightly. During the second verse I found myself on the receiving end of the full wrath of this venomous piece of hired equipment.

During my frantic setting up, I had decided on one hanging tom-tom only. Good thing really, as on top of everything else that was re-occurring, the fittings that held the tom in place got bored and stopped working. The drum now began to turn downwards so that its skin was at right angles to my snare drum, which had by now wandered back into my crotch.

Not to be left out of the fun, the drum stool decided to do its party piece and slip down a couple of notches. As I was getting to grips with my new seating arrangement, the crash cymbal literally crashed into a vertical alignment with the stand, courtesy of a broken wing nut.

Take two highly accomplished guitarists, a highly experienced bass player, and then put Charlie Chaplin on drums and you have pretty much the right picture of how this was shaping up. You could forgive anybody listening from the bar for thinking that the drummer was hallucinating, or that someone's child had been promised a go on the drums. I felt as though I had become some kind of amateur drum tech thrown in the deep-end of an exam in emergency mechanical logistics while the others played their instruments. The rest of the set continued in much the same catastrophic fashion.

At one stage, Murph, Texas Flood's bass player and great personal friend, came over to the kit and said: 'Spike! Do something – it's affecting everything!'

'Oh sorry! I was only having a laugh. I'll stop messing around and do it properly from now on...'

I was, however, flattered when someone came up afterwards and said something along the lines of, 'Nice one, mate. Like the way you kept it simple. You know, leaving all the flash stuff to the other guys.'

Yep, that's me. Never one to paradiddle myself out of a tight spot.

So you see, there are times when a reasonably good workman can justifiably blame his tools. It seems that drummers occupy a lower ground in the perception of some individuals whose job it is to provide hired equipment. Certainly, people who don't actually play the drums tend to know very little about how they actually work. They're just things you hit, aren't they?

If you're on tour in a well-known band with proper management, the chances are you'll have a drum tec to look after all your equipment requirements and he'll probably be a drummer himself. But when you're not at that level things can get a bit scary.

My experience was perhaps understandable because the whole event was for charity, but John Lingwood recalls an incident where something similar occurred and it certainly wasn't for charity. John's band, The Company Of Snakes (Whitesnake revisited) were supporting Alice Cooper in St Petersburg. There had been a power cut and the bands did not have the chance to check their equipment until half an hour before the gig was due to start, by which time the punters were already in the auditorium.

John had asked the hire people on the Russian leg of the tour to provide him with a Yamaha maple custom drum kit. When John was finally able to get to the hired kit he was horrified to find what looked like an assortment of old garden rubbish. In fact, it was an extremely old and knackered beginner's drum set that had probably been lying in the basement of a Russian youth club for decades.

The only remote connection with John's request was the fact that it had 'Yamaha' written on the bass drum batter head. After some frantic running around, John managed to nail the bass drum to the riser, assemble the toms as best he could and borrow a spare snare drum, cymbals and necessary hardware from Alice Cooper's drummer.

The problem with being a drummer is that while most good ones can adapt to different drum kits fairly easily, if you end up faced with a contraption that is completely antiquated and falling apart, you really do have a problem. But make no mistake: it will be your fault. Every time.

SECTION 14

FAME

Most Drummers Want More Than
Their Fifteen Minutes...

Most people, especially musicians, at some stage wonder what it must be like to be famous. I wonder if famous musicians ever wonder what it must be like *not* to be famous. I have been playing drums for 40 years, the last ten of those without the intention of becoming famous. I don't play enough these days, but when I do I enjoy it more than ever before. Still, I think there will always be a part of me that wonders what it would be like to play a stadium. Many of the great players featured in this book know only too well what it's like to play stadiums – they spend a great portion of their lives doing it.

Of course, getting your first taste of success doesn't necessarily involve giving up the day job.

CURTAINS

Imagine you live in a large house in a pleasant, leafy suburb and you are currently having it refurbished. It's Thursday, early evening and you are trying to watch TV. There's a young, rock 'n' roll type hanging curtains in your expansive, expensive living room and it involves a great deal of banging. This interferes with your concentration but, hey, it's only *Top of the Pops* and you're not mad keen on what's in the charts anyway.

Suddenly your attention is drawn to one of the bands on the screen. You quite like the track but something grabs you about the drummer. He looks strangely familiar but you just can't place him. It's as if you know him personally. You remark out loud: 'Hey, that's weird. I'm sure I know that bloke on the drums.'

You turn to see if the rock 'n' roll type has registered your remark. Strangely, the banging has stopped and he is perched atop his stepladder, hammer in hand, staring at the screen, completely transfixed. Then it clicks. You do a double take and realise with amazement that the drummer on the TV is actually the young workman in your front room – the curtain fitter. He's clearly the same person.

He laughs, shakes his head and says: 'You know what? It really wasn't meant to be like this...'

As it happened it wasn't curtains for the rock n roll type, whose name is Steve Grantley. The record was a hit and he soon went on to become a much sought after professional drummer. He now plays with both Stiff Little Fingers and The Alarm.

When a band first gets a taste of success, it's bound to be the drummer who's still doing the day job. Why? Because if you haven't written the song that's got you in the charts (and drummers usually haven't), you won't be getting an advance on publishing royalties. And you can wait forever to get what you're owed for mere performance royalties.

CLOSE BUT NO CIGAR

An English teacher, guitarist and composer; two professional violin players; a rock cellist; a backing singer and care worker; a Cher lookalike divorcee from Detroit on bass; a bloke from advertising on drums (me) and a French-Algerian deputy headmaster and Conservative candidate on congas.

This was Speaking In Tongues – a band I played with in back in the early '90s. The music was as diverse as the assembly of musicians. It was the first fusion of Arabic melodies, African dance rhythms and Western rock guitar to hit the London scene. And yes, I am doing a bit of setting the record straight here, as the songwriter and leader of the band, Keith Clouston, was indeed the first person to have the idea when he was working as an English teacher in the Sudan in the early '80s.

As a band we became very popular playing places like The Mean Fiddler, Subterrania and The Borderline, just off Charing Cross Road. It was the first time this style of music had been introduced to London and it caught on. We recorded a trance/dance cover version of Cream's 'I Feel Free', which was played at a lot of alternative discos around London. Naturally, we all thought that this would propel us to fame and fortune because we were on to something completely new.

One Friday night in 1991 we were due to play The

Borderline, supported by a single act from the States who was also reputed to be something completely new. We set up our gear on the small stage that afternoon, did a sound check, and then began the long stretch of hanging around for hours before the gig. This customary boredom was interrupted by the arrival of several burly roadies carrying a mini-grand piano, followed by a petite, attractive woman. We were asked to move our equipment to the back of the stage to accommodate both the piano and Tori Amos, who was to be our support that evening.

We had never heard of her and made a point of watching her from the dressing room area at the side of the stage. She was totally different and had an amazing ability to command an audience. More than 300 people crammed into that sweaty basement fell completely silent as she sang 'Silent All These Years' without even touching the piano. You could have heard a pin drop.

As luck would have it, our set was equally diverse but so different that the two acts, by coincidence, complemented each other very nicely. After a great gig we chatted with her in the bar and she wished our band good luck. Likewise, we wished her a successful future – something she went on to have in no small measure.

We, of course, didn't enjoy any further success. A year later we disbanded, and shortly after Jah Wobble and bands like Transglobal Underground had a series of chart hits with exactly the kind of music we had been playing. Many other acts have enjoyed success with East/West dance fusion permutations since.

In fact, Jah Wobble used to come to some of our gigs. I'm

saying nothing more, except that having secured a record deal with Warner Bros years later, our cellist eventually found out that they had been among several large record companies who had been 'queuing' up to sign us – but couldn't get hold of us! So instead, they signed a solo artist who was doing the same kind of stuff but using samples instead of a band, which turned out to be cheaper for them anyway.

So Speaking In Tongues were another band that got close but no cigar at the end of the day. Still, it turned out that our French-Algerian conga player had got on so well with Tori Amos that he managed to get a free backstage pass at her Royal Albert Hall performance. We put it down to him having the gift of the gab. Well, he was a Conservative candidate.

For most drummers, their first proper gig is often at school. You form a band with people of roughly the same age and play in the school hall, either at a school event or a specially organised concert promoted by your mates and a couple of trendy English teachers. It's going to be a nerve-racking experience because you will be watched by kids from the school, some teachers and maybe even your parents. The last thing you want to do is cock it up...

THE RIGHT PLACE AT THE WRONG TIME

Mike Wade's drumming career reached a pinnacle back in the '70s, when he played with The New Seekers. The band had had six Top 10 hits, the gigs were pretty easy and Mike had a close-up view of Lyn Paul's delightful derriere for an hour every night. But things hadn't always been this good for him...

I'm in the wings stage right in the school hall. It's almost time to take the stage. It's my first gig as a drummer at the tender age of 16 and I'm really nervous. Why? Because I can't play the drums properly. OK, I can keep a beat with the sticks, but I haven't got the hang of the feet side of things. I haven't practised enough to get them to behave independently of my arms. Until now I've only had a snare drum and cymbal to practise on. My dad has bought me a proper kit for the occasion, but I've never played it before. I should have said something before but felt too embarrassed. My lack of ability is now my own guilty secret.

There's been quite a build up to our little appearance at the school ball and there are loads of people out there in the audience: mums, dads, teachers, my mates. I can hear the head teacher's voice as he announces our band and the curtain opens.

Oh well, here goes.

At first, I keep my head down as we crash into our first number. I stamp down on both the hi-hat pedal and the bass drum pedal simultaneously and hope for the best. At least my time keeping's OK. After a while I can't resist looking up into the audience to gauge the reaction.

Oh dear. They don't look at all impressed. In fact, they look seriously pissed off. Most of them are looking at the floor! Come on, I'm not that bad.

Then I notice a couple of women starting to cry. Then one

of them actually faints. Really. I'd never have believed my performance could have that bad an effect.

Then the house lights go up, the curtains close and the show is stopped. Backstage, the head teacher comes in and has a word: 'Sorry lads, I think you'd better go home. Leave all your gear here – you can pick it up tomorrow.'

We can't quite believe this reaction, but have no choice but to leave quietly by the stage door and go our separate ways. When I arrive at home my mum opens the front door as I'm walking up the path – and she's in tears as well!

Wow, bad news travels fast. Am I going to be punished for this?

Then my Dad has a word with me.

I was right about the bad news travelling fast.

Seconds before the headmaster had introduced our band, he had announced something else. He'd just heard on the wireless that President Kennedy had been assassinated.

As you can imagine, I was ecstatic.

FIRST DAY ON THE JOB

Andy Burrows got the job as Razorlight's drummer through an audition back in early summer 2004. The original drummer had left a couple of months earlier. Being a writer/keyboard player as well, he contributed significantly to the band's material, co-writing songs like 'America' and 'Before I Fall to Pieces'. After five years, in May 2009, he left for 'personal reasons'. During the latter part of his time with Razorlight, Andy recorded and released a solo album, *The Colour of My Dreams*, to raise money for a children's hospice in his hometown of Winchester. Andy is now signed to

Universal Records, which is Razorlight's label, and has recently joined We Are Scientists.

When Andy got the job to tour with Razorlight, he was living in Winchester. He was, in fact, a country bumpkin, as he puts it. So going to London to rehearse would have been pretty exciting...

I'm on the train heading back home to Winchester. I've just finished four days of rehearsals with Razorlight in a top London studio. It's been intense but all has gone well and I'm fully prepared for the tour. I know the songs, my drum kit's all sorted, complete with plenty of spare sticks, skins and accessories. Physically I'm totally fit and well. And mentally I just can't wait.

I know I won't have to wait too long as I'm only home for tomorrow and the next day we're off. A real sense of well being comes over me. Well, I have treated myself to a few celebratory drinks during my journey back into the countryside. Contentedly, I lean back into my seat and find myself drifting effortlessly away...

The next thing I know I'm lying in a pile of rubble with blood, cuts and bruises all down my right side. A concerned station porter, along with some other kind people, help me to my feet. I am in quite a state physically and a state of shock, but soon I remember what happened.

I had fallen completely asleep on the train and nearly missed my stop. When I awoke the train was just starting to pull out of Winchester station. I knew I had to get off because otherwise I'd have ended up in Southampton. As luck would have it (or not, depending on how you look at it), this was an old-style train. It had those old-fashioned slam doors that aren't automatic, so I was able to grab my things and leap off the moving train.

The trouble was, my carriage had already passed the point where the end of the platform begins to slope down towards the rail track. And this particular slope is extremely steep. I end up spending the next day undergoing not inconsiderable repair work courtesy of the NHS in Winchester hospital.

And so Andy began his first tour with a major band covered in bruises and with aching limbs. The incident even made the tabloid press. In fact, he tells most of his outings in the press have been in some way related to injury or violence, and wants to make it clear that this is not an accurate reflection of the drummer in question.

SMASHING AUDITION

When I interviewed Nigel Glockler of Saxon he told me about an audition he went to back in his early days as a drummer. It was around 1975 and Nigel had answered an ad in the back of *Melody Maker* for a drummer to join a band influenced by The Rolling Stones and The New York Dolls, called London SS.

Being heavily into the Dolls and such bands (he'd even had a pair of boots identical to those worn by Doll drummer Jerry Nolan on their first album cover, made at Kensington market), he went up to meet them in a cafe in Paddington.

So I'm in this café waiting to meet them. A couple of them are walking around in leopard skin print trousers, pink belts etc and they certainly look the part. As I look around I can see quite a few other people here after the job. Eventually we get talking and I get the impression they like me because I'm talking about all the US bands they mentioned, like MC5, Flamin' Groovies and The Stooges.

A few days later I'm ensconced in a studio in Mornington Crescent (I think), playing through some stuff. Then they ask if I know 'Slow Death' by The Flamin' Groovies and could I emulate a car crash in the middle of the song please? A strange request but I can hardly refuse – it is an audition, after all.

So, as I get to the middle of the song I'm thinking, 'What do I do to sound like a car crash? Hit lots of crash cymbals at random, interspersed with chaotic tom tom abuse? Nah!'

Sod it, here goes. I crash a cymbal, then push it over. I kick the floor tom sideways. Then it's the hi-hat's turn – over it goes. Then my boot makes contact with the top of the bass drum and propels it forwards, taking the rack toms with it, into the middle of the studio floor. In short, I completely annihilate the kit. And I'm thinking, 'Actually, that felt pretty good.'
I look up to see my auditioners staring at me open mouthed. Then the band's manager comes into the studio and they all go off for a chat. I'm thinking they're figuring out what to charge me for the damage. After what seems like ages they all come back into the studio.

'We've all thought about it and we'd like you to join the band.'

I tell them I'll think about it and get back to them tomorrow. I give the lead guitarist a lift back to Crawley. As we're chatting, I'm having second thoughts. They're great guys and it would be right up my street, but something's nagging at the back of my mind.

So next day I give them a call and decline the gig, saying I honestly feel I'm not ready to turn pro just yet and apologise for wasting their time.

The guitarist was Brian James, who went on to The Damned. The bass player was Tony James, who went on to Generation X. The other guitarist was Mick Jones, who formed The Clash. And the manager, the guy who offered me the job, was Bernie Rhodes, who went on to manage The Clash. I can't remember who the singer was, but it certainly wasn't Billy Idol.

Later on, after I'd joined Toyah, I met Tony at a studio party and we had a good laugh about it all. Then I found out that Brian was living one minute from me in Brighton – he's now moved along the coast a bit.

Also, I've just seen an early history of Generation X online and Tony mentions shooing a drummer from Brighton away for not looking the part! Well, Tony, you know that's not true, but I guess it made good reading at the time!

All musicians are likely to meet some strange and eccentric characters on their travels, especially when they're on their way to the top. Drummers seem to attract the attention of these individuals more than anyone else.

ON THE WAY UP

Dylan Howe of The Blockheads told me about an audition he went to back in the early days when he was just starting out as a pro.

It's the early '90s and I'm in Terminal Studios at London Bridge, auditioning for a band called – wait for it – Fast Freddie's Fingertips. We've just started the third number when I notice a tall, middle-aged man with jet-black hair letting himself into the studio. He is quite an imposing figure as he comes over and stands right in the middle of the room. He's looking at something in his hand. As we carry on playing he glances up at us, scanning the band somewhat unsmilingly, and then back at the thing in his hand.

The song finishes and I think it's actually gone OK, even though the presence of this new person in the room has slightly thrown the atmosphere. I wait for some feedback or, hopefully, approval. The group's manager (a rather flamboyant individual who could make Arthur Daly look like Gandhi) then introduces me to the mysterious man with the gadget, who says: 'Nice to meet you. Well, when you first started playing, it was at 126bpm, and by the time you finished, it was at 128bpm.''

I don't know if this speed analysis was a good or bad thing at that time but I ended up doing quite a few gigs with Fast Freddie. I think it had cost our manager around £20,000 to buy us onto the tour [supporting Cher]. So there I was, in my early twenties, playing in these huge barns. Until then I had only ever dreamed about what a huge auditorium looked like from a drum riser. Of course, there were drawbacks – sharing B&B rooms with single beds and no hot water. Plus it seemed a little ironic that we're playing to between 10,000–15,000 people, but only being paid £30 a gig, which is what we we'd been getting for pub gigs in Crawley and Redhill before the tour.

I might have complained a bit about this, but at the end of

the day I was just thrilled to play in these places and to be on tour. I can honestly say I learned a lot in those days and I don't regret a minute of it. Sometimes you have to rough it while others reap the rewards of their own hard work. And as Miles Copeland would say: 'It's just not your table.'

As it turned out, the mysterious man in the studio was Dave Robinson who had signed the band to the legendary Stiff Records. Nice of him to drop in. And good point on the timing. Personally I usually try and keep the speed to within a maximum of 0.5 variable beats per minute. Anything more than that and it starts to get a bit scary, especially at auditions when you've gotta have your finger on the pulse big time.

Most drummers have their heroes from an early age. Even those who become successful in their own right still have a respect and even a reverence for the pop stars who inspired them in their youth. So when you finally get to meet them, or better still actually play with them, it's going to be a nerve-racking experience, however good you've become...

JUST FOR ONE DAY

Brett 'Buddy' Ascott was the drummer with mod revival group The Chords during the late 1970s and early '80s. They enjoyed several Top 75 hits and a Top 30 album, culminating in a *Top of the Pops* appearances and sell-out tours. Since The Chords split up, Buddy has played with many bands (including current project Pope), but has yet to repeat that early success. He was, however, chosen as the drummer for the 2005 charity reworking of The Small Faces' hit 'Watcha

Gonna Do About It'? for the Boxing Day tsunami victims, appearing alongside Ronnie Wood and PP Arnold.

But for Buddy, the real highlight of his career occurred one night in July 2009, when he drummed with some of his all time heroes: Mick Jones of The Clash, Glen Matlock of the Sex Pistols and Steve Diggle of Buzzcocks. He had dreamed of sharing a stage with them ever since he first came across punk as a teenager...

It's 28 November 1976 and I'm a bored 17-year-old, watching Sunday afternoon TV. The LWT show is featuring a Punk Rock Special with a short clip of the Sex Pistols playing live at the Notre Dame Hall, Leicester Square. I'd read about them in the *NME*, but never seen or heard them. I'm mesmerised. It is easily the most frightening, disturbing, threatening and exciting performance I've seen since early footage of The Who and I am instantly a fan.

Three days later the Pistols appear on the *Bill Grundy Show*, and the world is suddenly a different place.

Six months later, on 9 May 1977. I'm at the Rainbow theatre, North London. On a bill topped by The Clash, the stellar support includes The Prefects, Subway Sect, Buzzcocks and The Jam. It's a life-changing evening. Buzzcocks play their twisted love vignettes with speed and precision, and The Jam display the strength and intensity that will make them the biggest band in Britain within a few years. But The Clash are something else altogether. Their maelstrom of thrashing guitars, angry choruses and total conviction persuade me that I should help in the demolition of three rows of seats upstairs.

A month later I am a drummer in a punk band – The Meat.

So Buddy was hooked on high energy drumming pretty early. Playing with The Chords brought success, but he never forgot his dream of playing alongside The Jam and The Clash. His chance to live that dream comes 32 years later when two benefit concerts are arranged for photographer and writer Terry Rawlings, who is seriously ill with cancer. Many musicians and friends have pulled together to organise the shows, the first in Whitechapel and the second at the 100 Club on Oxford Street.

The plan is for a supergroup to close the show at the 100 Club – punk royalty comprising Mick Jones of The Clash, the Sex Pistols' Glen Matlock, Steve Diggle of Buzzcocks and the erstwhile Kinks drummer Mick Avory. The Chords, with Jeff from The Purple Hearts, are due to play an early set there that night. I dream of sneaking onstage for the last number of the supergroup's set and inconspicuously bashing a tambourine on the peripheries. If only I had the guts...

We rehearse two Chords' songs, one by Purple Hearts' and an Undertones number. So far so good, so far so controllable, and so far – within my capabilities.

Come the big day, 26 July 2009, another Sunday. It's 3.22pm and I'm at home, about to bite into a sandwich. The phone rings. It's Jeff of The Purple Hearts calling from the depths of the 100 Club: 'Bud, Mick Avory hasn't turned up. Do you want to do a set with Matlock, Jones and Diggle tonight?'

'Err... yes please!'

'OK, I'll put Glen on....'

'Hello? Buddy? This is Glen. We're doing 'Should I Stay', 'Pretty Vacant', 'Train in Vain', 'All or Nothing' and 'Stepping Stone' – you up for it?'

'Err…what time?'

'Great! Get yourself over here…' The line goes dead.

It's one thing dreaming of performing on stage with your heroes, but when you actually get the chance, it's terrifying. Buddy's wife Hideko, who witnessed the call, said he actually dropped his sandwich and turned completely white.

After the call I fly into the bedroom and throw some T-shirts, two towels and a handful of drumsticks into a bag. Suddenly I'm struck by a terrifying thought: Do I know 'Pretty Vacant'? Can I actually play it? With the bloke who wrote it?

The problem with playing the drums is that it's not only physically demanding, it is the backbone to any rock/pop/punk song. Bands desperately need to be able to rely on a drummer's ability to provide that essential bottom line. A guest guitarist can quickly learn a few chords and just play a few twiddly bits. But a drummer? He has to get it right from the start.

The computer's still on, so I quickly find a video of the Pistols doing 'Pretty Vacant' on YouTube. I look round to see Hideko laughing hysterically. She has walked in to find me in just my pants, drumming along on the sides of my chair. It brings me to my senses. I realise I just haven't got time for this. I try to dress appropriately but can't find a razor blade to slash my shirt.

Just as I run to East Putney tube station Glen Matlock calls again: 'Buddy? Change of plan. We're doing a quick rehearsal. Do you know Mick's studio, under the Westway?'

'Sorry, I don't.'

'Come out of Ladbroke Grove tube, follow the Westway to Portobello Road – it's near there.'

'I'm on my way.'

Sitting on the steps at the station I realise I am shaking. Suddenly I'm tired, my back hurts and a wave of panic is running through me, sapping my energy and my confidence. Is this really happening? I ring Hidz who tells me the District line isn't running – AAARRGH!! She picks me up in the car and we set off to west London, via my storage unit to pick up some spare sticks. I envisage destroying half a forest of drumsticks trying to get to grips with these songs. As we approach the studio Matlock rings again: 'Where are you?'

'Just went past a KFC.'

'That means you've gone past us!'

Already Buddy has made a mistake and he hasn't sat down behind the kit yet. A drummer's perception of his fellow musicians changes dramatically when they suddenly consist of really famous people. So it's no surprise that Buddy's running round like someone just set fire to one of his farts.

Finally we spy the studio entrance. Brakes on, sticks out, and up the stairs before I have a chance to chicken out. Mick Jones is at the studio door. I blurt out a greeting: 'Hello! I haven't seen you since 1980!'

I don't know what reply I was expecting – perhaps something like: 'Oh yeah, I remember you – you played for The Chords when you beat The Clash at football in Hyde Park!' But of course not. Jones just continues smiling. That was how I'd always remembered him. A real sweetie.

Then Glen Matlock, business-like and eager to get on, hurries me into the rehearsal room. There my heart sinks. There is a drum kit – of sorts. A bass drum, a snare and two toms. That's it. No hi-hat. No stands, no cymbals. No bass drum pedal. Not even a stool!

Typical. Some rehearsal rooms are hopeless when it comes to equipment hire, but it's always the drum kits that are most lacking. It's as if the instrument is not regarded as particularly important. Just give the bloke something to hit and he'll be happy. For those who are not drummers, the missing elements here are essential components: you simply cannot play properly without them. OK, you can bash out a rhythm on what's available, like you would on a desk at school, but that's hardly playing the drums. Still, Buddy soldiers on.

'I'll... err... I'll get started then,' I cheerfully venture, thinking: 'How am I gonna impress them on this piece of junk?'

Steve Diggle arrives, a friendly and familiar face from numerous pubs around London. He looks only half as pensive as I feel. Matlock, clearly the leader of this motley collection, announces we'll start with 'Pretty Vacant'.

Good, I think, I'll just strip down to my pants then I should be able to remember it! We start relatively quietly, Matlock shouting out the chord changes and the arrangement. As we gather momentum and nail the song, we get louder and louder. Soon a small throng of curious onlookers gathers, gazing in through the glass door and the studio window. I swear I can lip read their faces: 'Look! That's Mick from The Clash – and Glen Matlock of The Jam! There's Diggle from the Buzzcocks! And that's... yeah, who the f*** is that on the drums? And where are the drums? He doesn't sound very good!'

We attempt 'Should I Stay or Should I Go' and I'm thankful that I'd at least played the song years ago with a band somewhere in Japan. Jonesy is grinning again. Eventually a drum stool appears, and then a pedal, and by playing on the drum rims I'm able to imagine myself playing on a whole kit. I am so relieved to sit down that I say: 'Right, that's the end of The Stray Cats set!' Nobody laughs, but I decide not to try to explain it. [The Stray Cats' drummer, Slim Jim, famously used to play standing up.] Mick sings, smokes, beams some more, drinks some beer, and looks like a happy man. Maybe I am doing OK. The other songs follow in quick succession.

After nearly an hour Matlock declares himself happy and my rehearsal time is finished. We haven't played all the songs, but I'll just have to wing the rest. So I'm out the door, across to the tube station where happily there are some trains running. At Oxford Circus I sit on a bench in the rain, trying to take stock of the situation. I eat a banana and call Hidz, but I am still shaking. It's not because of the drizzle.

Next stop, The 100 Club on Oxford Street, and after a quick acoustic rehearsal in the dressing room (if you can call it that) it's time for The Chords to take the stage. Our set is going down a storm and I'm building confidence for that grand finale later. But then disaster strikes. I put my foot straight through the bass drum.

There is one part of a drum kit that is impossible to replace quickly and that is the bass drum skin. And I have put my foot straight through it. I have never done this before, not in 30 years of gigging... so why tonight?!

The problem with drums is there is so much that can go

wrong. That's why drummers better-off touring bands have a drum tech, whose job it is to keep his eye on the kit and replace anything that breaks. No matter how much you spend on quality equipment, a skin can always break, a thread in a nut can go, a spring can come loose. But when you can't afford to pay a tech, breakages become a worry. Because, unlike replacing a guitar string, when something goes on the kit you've got to get all mechanical and clever – and fast. Of course, on this occasion there was no spare skin and, being a Sunday, all the drum shops are closed.

Mick Stoner – roadie to the stars, Bobby Davro lookalike and all-round good chap – saves the day, temporarily, as he patches up the broken skin with gaffer tape. We play 'Maybe Tomorrow', but the skin gives way again: 'Sorry chaps, the beast unleashed within me with this song will not allow a timid performance! I've bust the skin again.' Mick weaves his magic again and we finish our set with The Undertones' classic 'Teenage Kicks', joined by Damian O'Neill of the 'tones. As I leave the stage I turn to Mick: 'The skin's f***ed, mate. How's it gonna see out another three sets?'

Mick sets about repairing the pulverised skin with cardboard, plastic laminates – and a crushed-up Red Bull can! Perhaps his optimism and hard work may just pull us through. But later that evening, assuming it does hold out, the bass pedal will feel like I'm kicking a brick wall for 30 minutes, and days later the subsequent bruises will convince me I've broken a toe.

In an effort to cool down and rehydrate myself, I stand outside in the rainy street. I am not mobbed. Mick Jones and the others arrive, and are mobbed. Then Mick Avory arrives, the guy who was supposed to play the finale set in the first place! Surely he's not gonna steal my thunder, rain on my parade, piss on my chips?

Happily, no. Diplomacy prevails and it's decided Avory will play just the last number, The Kinks' 'You Really Got Me'. Well, I can't really quibble with that, can I? The man is a living legend and one of my all time favourite drummers. And a gentleman. And he does play on the record!

Next up is Steve Diggle's band. They deliver a sterling set, but by now I'm not paying much attention. I'm in a hyperactive state of fear, excitement and hysteria. I can't decide whether to run screaming from the club ('I can't do it! I can't do it, I tell you!') or simply faint on the spot. I'm certainly hot enough to faint – it's about 35 degrees down there and I haven't cooled down since the rehearsal five hours earlier.

I find myself at the side of the stage, propping up a fast-ailing Terry Rawlings as we help him onstage to deliver a heartfelt thank you to all concerned. He then hands over to Matlock, Jones and Diggle. They play a shambolic yet strangely affecting rendition of 'Debris', Jones constantly coming over to Terry and gently patting him, encouraging him, always smiling that infectious grin of his. I'm tearful and exuberant at the same time.

Suddenly I realise that I'm up next. It's like my bungy jump, my skydive, my white-water rafting is all before me again. All rolled into one huge pile of 'Oh my God – am I really going to do this?' But, as then, there's no escape, so I guess I'd best just enjoy it.

Matlock doesn't actually know my name so introduces me

as 'Mr Buddy' as I clamber onstage. I take my place, and Jones turns to me as I ask him: 'What are we starting with?'

'"Train in Vain".'

I realise I've never played it in my life.

'Mick – how's it go?'

'Oh, you know, a little skip intro and you're off.'

Then the memory of it starts to materialise from somewhere in the back of my mind. Not the most difficult intro or beat I've ever played, but I'm still a little unsure. Then Jones plays that riff, the one that sold The Clash to the USA, and the crowd cheers. Suddenly I know I can do it and it all falls into place.

And I can't take the smile off my face. In fact, I am almost laughing with joy. Not smugness, not arrogance, not hubris, just pure unadulterated happiness. For 20 minutes I am going to play some fantastic music with three absolute heroes of mine, to a surging crowd in one of the best venues in the world.

Wow.

At first I keep it straight, keep it simple. Don't take risks, I tell myself, don't take chances. It's not your kit, your songs, nor your audience. In fact, at this point, it doesn't even feel like your body!

I have Jones to my left, Matlock in front of me, and Diggle to my right. It's heaven. I'm in musical utopia. I can almost see myself from the opposite wall, from the mixing desk. I ask, 'Who's that up there with those stars?' I do not ponder, 'Who's that up there with Buddy?!'

And then... the best bit. I get comfortable; I get confident. I *can* do this!

The impish ghost of Keith Moon pops up in my mind, as he is wont to do at times of great temptation: 'Oh, go on, do a roll here, try that fill there, it'll be alright! What can go wrong?'

So I do. Outrageously at times. I start a roll miles too early and somehow manage to get back in time for the chorus. I think only Mick Stoner, and maybe Jeff from my band, are aware of the risks I'm taking, but as as I've got my own audience I might as well throw some other stuff in too. It all goes brilliantly. Soon we're into 'Pretty Vacant', followed by 'Should I Stay', and then the venerable 'All or Nothing'.

Nothing fazes me, nothing throws me, I don't drop or break a single stick. At the end of my final song, 'Stepping Stone', I do some flashy off-beat stuff on the snare and Matlock joins in, smiling all the way.

And then it's over.

I try to walk off, but Jones stops me to shake my hand. I'm aware that Mick Avory is getting up to play 'You Really Got Me', but has no sticks. I hand him mine, and walk to the bar for my first beer of the evening.

The plaudits and praise come non-stop, even from some green-eyed drummers in the audience. I wish to apologise to each and every one of them – Paul, Gary, Jim – for having had the good fortune to take part. But I can't stop smiling.

Dave Edwards, the DJ, comes up to me: 'Buddy – up there you looked like a baboon in a field of bananas!'

And a week later I still feel like that.

After nearly 40 years of wondering if I was good enough, I suppose I can finally believe that I am. That I was – at least for one night... Just for one day. Two days later I ring Terry, the guy the concert was in aid of. 'I know this might sound totally inappropriate, Terry, but I just wanted to say thank you for one of the best nights of my life.'

Drumming can be a frightening business, especially when you're playing unrehearsed with people you have looked up to all your musical life. I've never had the chance to jam or sit in with the likes of the Stones or any of my heroes. But if I did, I'd be panicking just like Buddy was. And would it be worth all that stress? You only have to read Buddy's sign off to know the answer to that.

There is usually a good deal of goodwill among drummers, just as there is usually a generous sprinkling of goodwill among most musicians, regardless of how famous they may be. Stuart Doughty, drummer with Reverend And The Makers, describes a brief encounter he had at a busy London venue some years ago:

I'm in this band called Seafruit and we're playing a gig in London. I load my drum kit through quite a busy bar and pile them in a corridor, as close to the stage as I can. I then set them up so all that's left to do is carry them on stage.

I begin with the bass drum. As I'm carrying it down the corridor near the bar I notice the passageway is blocked by a bloke and two girls. I'm thinking, 'Here we go again – another round of endless excuse me's and polite apologies.' As I approach, carrying my bass drum in front of me, I decide to be a little more authoritative:

'Watch yourself pal, coming through...'

Rather than stepping aside, the bloke turns round. It's Robbie Williams. I imagine there aren't many occasions on which Robbie Williams is told to get out of the way. He apologises and steps aside. Not only that, he then offers to help me load the rest of my drum kit onto the stage. As he's clambering on and off the stage with my stuff, I'm thinking this must be the first time the roadie has been infinitely more famous than the drummer.

And what a decent bloke.

SECTION 15

THE CODA CLUB

Drummers Who've Been There, Done It All And Got A Lot More Than A T-shirt...

A drian Macintosh, erstwhile drummer with the great Humphrey Lyttelton, once kindly invited me to a gathering of senior citizen jazz musicians. They meet every last Monday of the month in the basement bar of the Phoenix Theatre just off Charing Cross Road. They are part of a members-only organisation called The Coda Club, so named because most of them are fairly elderly.

I went along and was taken aback by their sheer enthusiasm for this book. I found myself talking to several drummers who had dozens of tales to tell about the old days before technology played such a huge role in modern music. Not just stuff like electronic drums, in-ear headphones, click tracks and so on, but also things like double bass drum pedals that automatically make every drummer sound faster and add a degree of thunderous dynamic to every modern drum solo.

One old gentleman, Joe Pawsey, told me how he and two other drummers played a solo for the Queen at The Royal

Command Performance. Rehearsing the three-minute piece for three weeks, they managed to achieve a completely synchronised three-drummer solo, played on three white drum kits on drum risers centre stage at The Palladium.

Never far from the bar, these old boys had a zest for life that clearly epitomised their happy memories of life as a drummer. Animated and with mischievous grins, they would reminisce with the kind of passion that can only come from an instrument that brings ultimate stimulation and satisfaction to whoever is lucky enough to take it up properly.

There was a big buzz in the Coda Club, a combination of humour and camaraderie that escalated as the booze flowed and the afternoon progressed. I got the feeling that this sense of comradeship had its roots not only in the shared joy of musicianship (in our case drumming) but also in a bygone age. A time when people pulled together for very different reasons, a social culture in which every moment of shared joy was ever more precious, a time when a sense of humour was as essential as your ration book.

I was chatting at the bar with Adrian when another elderly drummer entered. As he approached, Adrian caught his attention and introduced me. 'Spike here is writing a book of drummers' stories. I bet you've got plenty you could contribute!'

The old gentleman removed his coat and replied: 'Oh yes, plenty. I'm also very thirsty...'

I had met Adrian Macintosh himself some weeks earlier in Whitehall...

DANGLING THE CARROT

Adrian Macintosh played for the great Humphrey Lyttelton until the trumpet player's death in 2008. Adrian has also worked with many other jazz greats, including Sonny Stitt, Clark Terry, Teddy Edwards, Buddy Tate, Jiggs Whigham and Scott Hamilton. He is also featured on Radiohead's album, *Amnesiac*.

I actually saw him perform onstage with Lyttelton at the Watford Palace Theatre a few years ago. At that time I had only just begun to put this book together. Little did I know that I would be meeting him in person at the salubrious, very grand and beautiful National Liberal Club in London's Whitehall. This building also houses the Savage Club, where Adrian is honorary secretary. We sat in the quiet bar drinking fine red wine just a few feet away from Charlie Chaplin's famous walking stick, which rests in a thin, glass cabinet on the wall.

As well as drumming, Adrian's other loves include art, architecture, bird watching and walking. He told me about an incident some years ago that involved a vegetable…

Acker Bilk and his band were touring Australia. At one concert, as Acker was in his dressing room waiting for show time, a stranger popped in and played 'Stranger on the Shore' on a carrot. Acker was astonished as the chap gave him his card, which read: 'Col E Flower, Musical Fruit and Veg for your Entertainment'. The incident was related to a group of us by Acker some time later during a 30-concert tour of Britain featuring Acker's band, us (Humphrey Lyttelton band) and Kenny Ball and his band.

A few days later in Yorkshire I spotted a giant carrot on a market stall. I just had to have it. I purchased it and took it home. I borrowed a very long drill and drilled out the middle, making sure it was big enough to take a clarinet mouthpiece, and then added the holes for the octave key and notes of the scale.

Two days later we were all in Acker's dressing room, due onstage before a capacity crowd in Plymouth. Our sax player and clarinettist, Alan Barnes, put his clarinet mouthpiece in the carrot and, just for a joke, popped into Acker's dressing room and played 'Stranger on the Shore'.

All the musicians had joined us for the joke. Kenny Ball loved it and said, "You must play it in the finale,' which had all three bands on stage together playing Woody Herman's 'Woodchoppers Ball'. It worked a treat. Only the first few rows could actually see that the solo was being played on a carrot. The rest of the audience were completely mystified at this tiny instrument making all that noise.

Adrian told me that their concerts often get local reviews but little in terms of national music press. But on this occasion they did get a mention in the national press. It was in a national gardening magazine under an article entitled 'Unusual Things To Do With Vegetables'.

As we've seen already, avoiding serious injury is always a good idea, especially for a drummer. When it comes to avoiding everyday injuries, most musicians have to keep an eye on their fingers and/or their voices. But a drummer must take care of all his body parts: arms, legs, feet, fingers, head, ribs, the lot. So, from a practical point of view, a lot of recreational activities are potentially off limits...

BREAK A LEG

As previously mentioned, Adrian Macintosh's other loves include art, architecture, bird watching and walking...

I was on a walking holiday in Canada and America. On this occasion I had climbed to the ridge of the Valley of the Ten Peaks, above Moraine Lake in Alberta. We were on the way back down when suddenly I tripped and broke my ankle. I was in a lot of pain.

Two serious climbers approached and stopped to help. One gave me a painkiller while the other broke off a branch from a nearby tree and made me a crutch. They resumed their descent saying they would inform Mountain Rescue. However, by the time the helicopter arrived I had managed to hobble down into a wooded area and could not be seen, so I was left to make my own way back down.

This was at the beginning of a three-week walking and climbing holiday, which was now clearly going to become a sightseeing holiday, with my wife Sheila doing all the driving. But what really worried me was that on my return I was due to play with Humphrey's band at the Brecon and Edinburgh festivals.

Before returning home we stayed with some friends in Toronto. While I was there I took the opportunity to pop into the local drum store to try out some hi-hat pedals. Luckily I was able to operate the pedals without too much difficulty. I was fortunate that it was my left ankle that was broken as the bass drum pedal would probably be too much to ask. On returning to England, I told Humph the news...

'You've done what?'

'Broke my ankle, sorry.'

'You'd better be able to play – these festivals are good gigs."

But true to character, Humph saw an opportunity for a joke. Announcing my name each night at Brecon and Edinburgh, the band played a different tune relating to my ankle. 'I've Got a Feeling I'm Falling' and 'Climb Every Mountain' are two that spring to mind.

As we've seen before, being a working drummer involves taking care of one's body. So why is it that drummers tend to be the people who love all the dangerous stuff? Adrian told me that from then on Humph always joked that there should be a special clause in his contract forbidding him to climb mountains. I strongly suspect that his worries about his drummer's ability to play were peppered with a genuine concern for Adrian's health as a friend. But the fact remained that the problem of a drummer with a passion for mountain walking was not going to go away...

AVALON

The Humphrey Lyttelton band was on a trip to the Hong Kong Festival. We were lucky enough to have a day off so the bass player, Paul Bridge, myself and our wives decided to get up early and do some sightseeing, hiking up into the mountains for an exploratory day out. Eventually we reached a monastery which was open to tourists and decided to have a look around, and while there had a simple Buddhist lunch. Afterwards we climbed back down the mountain path and returned wearily to the hotel and told Humph what a great day we had enjoyed. I knew by his expression he was not impressed as his day had been fairly dull. It would have been wiser to keep quiet.

Later that night, during our performance at the Hong Kong Hilton, he decided to test my stamina in the finale of the show, which to my dismay was one of my least favourite numbers, a song called 'Avalon'. He featured it as a drum solo and having had a long day I realised that he was getting his revenge, knowing that I would be knackered. When it got to the drum solo, I played one chorus and Humph signalled one more, watching for me to disintegrate.

Just as the rigor mortis began to settle in, Humph signalled grandly for another drum chorus, before raising his trumpet for the final chorus. He was smiling all the way through, revelling in the fact that I could do nothing about it.

There's nothing worse. You're playing a particularly difficult drum pattern on stage and suddenly it's decided that it's time for the drummer to start soloing, thus displaying your skill and affinity with that particular style. This rarely happens in pop or rock bands as drum solos are usually planned or simply don't feature in the set. But in jazz, it's a tradition that the bandleader will offer solos to the other band members throughout the show, so it was easy for Humph to take his revenge on Adrian for his earlier gallivanting in the hills.

Adrian told me that ever since that day he has hated

Avalon even more and it had always lurked there as a possibility if Humph wanted to keep him in check. All he had to say was, 'I think we'll play Avalon' and Adrian ran for cover. He also said that since that day the name Avalon has cropped up frequently...

Two years ago we were in Los Angeles and when a friend of ours on the local session scene found out that we were to be in Long Beach for a few days, he said: 'You must visit Catalina Island.' We did and discovered the name of the main town where we docked was Avalon.

Last year in New York we ended up staying in the Avalon Hotel and when out for the day and looking for a drug store what did we find but – you've guessed it – the Avalon drug store.

To top it all I was born in Tadcaster, in a house called... Avalon.

MIND YOUR L'S AND R'S

At the Coda Club I also met an interesting chap called Roy Holliday. He told me that his experiences as a musician were to a large extent unremarkable, but his association with the Pearl drum company as principal endorsement agent in England had had its amusing moments...

My relationship with Pearl and my Japanese taskmasters was unique. For such a technically advanced nation it was a surprise to find the huge difference in their culture and understanding of the English language. I vividly remember my relationship with the Japanese senior management at

Pearl. They would always begin an inquiry with 'Loy San', which is their equivalent of Mr or Sir Roy, but the polite formalities tended to stop there. For instance, if we wanted to ask them to do something, we would say something like: 'Would it be possible for you to...?' Whereas they would simply issue a curt order.

I once received a call with a request in the matter of endorsement artists. Usually, calls from Pearl would be taken at my London office. However, on this occasion they had obviously been discussing the matter at some length and called me at the end of their working day, about six o'clock in the evening in Japan, and roughly two in the morning our time. So I was woken suddenly at home in the middle of the night by the phone ringing. Wearily, I picked up the receiver to hear a shrill Japanese voice.

'Loy San, you get Phil Corrins.'

'Er, pardon?'

'Phil Corrins! You get Phil Corrins!'

'Well, the thing is...'

'And Loger Tayror! You get Phil Corrins and Loger Tayror!'

I tried to explain that people who play for groups like Genesis and Queen had most likely made their choice of drum kit many years ago based on very specific individual requirements and a good deal of personal taste, but the Japanese insisted we contact them and persuade them to switch to Pearl drums.

In fact we did sign Phil Collins, not because of his particular liking for our product, but because we made a small size replica drum set for his young son. We were not so successful with Loger Tayror. I personally pursued this one for several months but we didn't move the Queen drummer from Ludwig.

Roy also remembers several incidents in which the confusion of two letters 'R' and 'L' – which are essentially the same in Japanese – caused some embarrassment...

In 1981 the company invested money in a drumstick operation to make Pearl sticks. After the first production run, they proudly presented me with the new drumstick. On closer examination of this very good product I discovered next to the Pearl logo, in bold letters, 'AMELICAN HICKOLY'. This was prominently displayed on every stick. Needless to say they were sold only in Japan.

On another occasion the US Pearl operation had signed an endorsement deal with the famous jazz drummer Art Blakey. On a subsequent visit to Japan I was shown some publicity material featuring his name as 'Art Brakey'. After some persuasion the Japanese were made aware of the error. The next day I was shown the new copy which now read 'Art Blackey'.

WHY I OUGHTA...

It was in one of my local pubs, The Unicorn in Abbots Langley, that I was fortunate enough to be introduced to an older gentleman, 24 years my senior. His name is Paul Hughes and he plays bass guitar. However, it is Paul's connection with the drummer featured in this tale which is significant here. We chatted and Paul shed some light on what it was like being in a pop band when it all started back in the early '60s.

There were no rehearsal studios in those days, so bands used scout huts, trade union halls and the like in which to practise. My band, The Mountain Kings, used to rehearse on Monday nights at the Territorial Army Drill Hall in Watford. We had an audience who paid sixpence to get in and watch the band rehearse while buying drinks at the bar. The deal was that if we wanted to go over a number twice they'd have to put up with it, but because the whole scene was so new it didn't matter. Bands were always lending each other musicians so the chances were there'd be someone in the audience who had played with you before anyway. It was quite easy to sit in with bands because they all played covers of established hits. Making up your own songs was unheard of back then.

Things seems to have come full circle to a degree. Pubs are putting cover bands on all the time these days, and musicians get shared around just like then. I'm currently one of three drummers who get moved around in several different bands. Anyway, the point Paul is making is that in the beginning, because pop music was a relatively new phenomenon, there was a strong sense of community and fraternity among musicians. Then one night Keith Moon turned up.

In those days there was a 48-hour working week, so if you were in a band as well, things could get a bit busy. I would get up at 7.30, cycle to work for an 8am start as an apprentice toolmaker, leave work at five and cycle back home. Mum would have dinner ready, then at seven in the evening Dad would load the band's gear into his ice cream van (The 'Eldorado'), pick up the rest of the band and drive us to wherever the gig was. Sometimes it was London, other times it was somewhere on the south coast.

The journey was a tad uncomfortable. The driver's seat wasn't bolted to the floor and the passenger seat was an old crate with a couple of cushions on top. The rest of the band would be in the back leaning against the fridge. But it didn't bother myself, my dad or the others. A gig was a gig and that was the main thing. We wouldn't normally get back until three in the morning, so it was about four hours sleep and then up again for work. But nobody minded; that's how it was in those days.

One night, we were due to perform at Elstree Film Studios as part of a Christmas party especially arranged for the studio staff. Two bands had been booked for the evening, Clyde Burns And The Beachcombers were headlining and The Mountain Kings were doing the support slot. So imagine the scene. Two over excited young pop bands are gathered, with their girlfriends at Elstree studios, taking it in turns to have a brief run-through before the evening begins.

Clyde Burns And The Beachcombers are doing fairly well so they are the logical choice to headline. They are set up at the back of the stage, which features an enormous drum riser with a huge drum kit. It's a Premier, which was an even bigger name in those days, and it belongs to their drummer, a certain Keith Moon. It should be noted that Mr Moon is only 17 at the time and relatively unknown. Our drummer Kevin's drum kit, an old Broadway make, is set up beside Keith's and looks very small and dinky in comparison. Still, our drummer's only 14, and he can't be expected to have a big Premier kit at that age.

There's a lot of milling about and general chit chat going on, then it's time for us to have a quick sound check before they open the doors and the audience drifts in. We go on stage and start playing. It all seems to be fine, except for one thing. Keith Moon is watching us, clearly in his element as he mimics Kev's playing. He's completely taking the piss. It's not as though Kev deserves it. He's not a bad drummer for 14, in fact. He's just not lucky enough to have a massive kit with loads of drums to show off on.

I'm especially angered by this because Kev is going out with my sister and I feel a bit protective. However, there's no time to say anything after our run-through because we're due on almost straight away. We do our set, which goes down well. Backstage during the interval I decide to have a word with Mr Moon: 'Listen mate, there was no need for that...'

'What?'

'Taking the mick out of our drummer during rehearsal. OK, so his kit's not as good as yours but what does that matter? He's only 14...'

'Would you like to discuss this outside?'

Apparently Mr Moon was not actually as polite as that. This incident happened long before he had acquired the well-spoken 'Dear boy' voice. On this occasion he was still a North London lad from Wembley.

So next thing I know we're scuffling about in the car park, throwing punches and rolling around on the ground in front of 'Eldorado'. Then suddenly, without warning, Keith Moon gets up, dusts himself down and wipes some blood from his face. 'I'm really sorry but I'd better get on stage now...'

'Oh yes, of course...'

'OK, well, I'll see you later...'

He has a bleeding nose and I have a black eye. But incredibly, we shake hands.

Tales of Keith Moon often reveal a sense of acting: it's as though he is constantly playing a part. The sudden realisation that he had to go on stage meant that the game was over for the time being, and he had a job to do. Shaking hands would have been almost like saying 'Thanks, I enjoyed that.' In fact, it's well known that Keith often enjoyed fencing with his next-door neighbour, Oliver Reed. But what is more poignant is that this story is another example of the kind of gentleman's approach to social conflict so affectionately associated with a world long since past.

And it's my belief that if any member of a band is going to offer the hand of friendship after a fight, it'll most likely be the drummer.

DOUBLE BUBBLE

Eddie Clayton has already appeared in this book. He is a fine jazz drummer and friend of mine. Although not a member himself, he knows many of the members of the Coda Club, so I thought it fitting to include this story, which again illustrates a drummer's determination to get the job done, whatever the circumstances.

The setting is the early '70s, somewhere in Southall. I've been booked to play as a duo with a Hammond organ player in a social club. At around 7pm I arrive at the club and slowly start setting up my drum kit. I'm feeling relaxed and looking forward to it. I've never been to the club before and have never met the organ player, but that's no problem. These kind of gigs turn up every now and then. You simply establish a rapport with the other musician(s) and wing it.

After half an hour or so I've got the drums all sorted. There's no sign of the organist yet so I grab the opportunity for a pint at the bar. I take a look around the place. There are a few early birds sitting at tables around the edge of the room on high-backed bench seats. The rest of the place is still fairly empty. A couple of bar flies are propping up the bar. I spy the tiny, uncarpeted wooden floor area in the middle of the room, reserved for later on when people are juiced up and brave enough to dance, and wonder if we'll manage to get anyone up tonight.

Half an hour slips by and still no sign of the organist. I order another pint thinking that'll have to be it until the interval. I need to stay fairly alert as I don't know what songs we'll be playing. People are starting to drift in now. Families, a few lads, plus a group of girls who already seem fairly well oiled – in fact, it looks like it might be a hen night because one girl is wearing a tiara. Anyway, it's filling up. But still no sign of the organ player. I'm starting to get a bit concerned.

I decide to ask the landlord what time we're due to start. He says about 15 minutes! He seems equally surprised the organist hasn't showed up and gives her a call. No reply. Maybe she's on her way? Apparently she doesn't live far away.

Another half hour goes by and, although the club is quite full and people are busy chatting, I see them looking over expectantly at my drums. Well, I need the money, so I've got to do something. So I decide to do a little solo to keep them happy. I get a few whoops and claps as I get behind the kit. They seem like a good crowd. I launch into my standard solo routine as the clientele cheer me on. I finish with a few elaborate cymbal crashes to loud applause. The punters seem to love it. They are actually shouting for more. It's as though they were only expecting a drummer on this particular night.

I start another solo, this time with a different rhythm and tempo on the tom toms. I improvise, progressing it through to another frenzied ending. Again, more applause. But still no organist. I'm thinking they'll get fed up with it if I do yet another solo. But I can't just stop and saunter back to the bar – whoever heard of a social club evening consisting of two drum solos?

There's a microphone set up just by the seemingly redundant organ for the would-be organist to sing into. I decide to commandeer it, so I place the mike and stand next to my hi-hat. I've never delivered a drum lecture before but I figure if ever there was a time to start...

'Ladies and gentlemen, boys and girls...' I decide to demonstrate different styles of drumming. I try to copy people like Gene Krupa and pop drummers like Dave Clarke from The Dave Clarke Five. I even raise my sticks up high like Dave Clarke to create his individual 'high stroke' approach. The punters seem to be taking it all in. Not exactly what they're used to but it seems that's no bad thing. But my impromptu drumming lecture has to finish somewhere, so once again I'm at a loss as what to do next.

And of course, still no organist. I decide to take a break. While I'm sitting at the bar, I notice that people are chatting animatedly and looking over. The landlord comes up and says can I carry on? I get back behind my kit without the faintest idea what to do next. Then I have another idea.

'Can anyone here play the drums? Would anyone like to try?' The next half hour turns into a kind of drum clinic for non-drummers. Some of the lads have a bash, then some young kids, even Auntie Flo. Then an old boy gets up and does a turn with an out-of-tune kazoo. Uncle Ron gets up to tell a few jokes.

I end up hosting an entire evening of light entertainment put on largely by the club punters themselves. The rest of the evening is a kind of free-for-all bonanza. I finish with one more drum solo. The club love it and everyone leaves shaking my hand as they go. The landlord pays me my full amount as the last punter leaves. Then he says he thought it very strange the organist didn't turn up. Still, he doesn't know her personally so I might as well have her share as well. So I get paid twice. Oh, and before I go: 'Do you work in your own duo?'

'Yes, sometimes...'

'Would you like a residency here at the club?'

'Yeah, that would be great!'

'What sort of duo is it?'

'Drums and organ.'

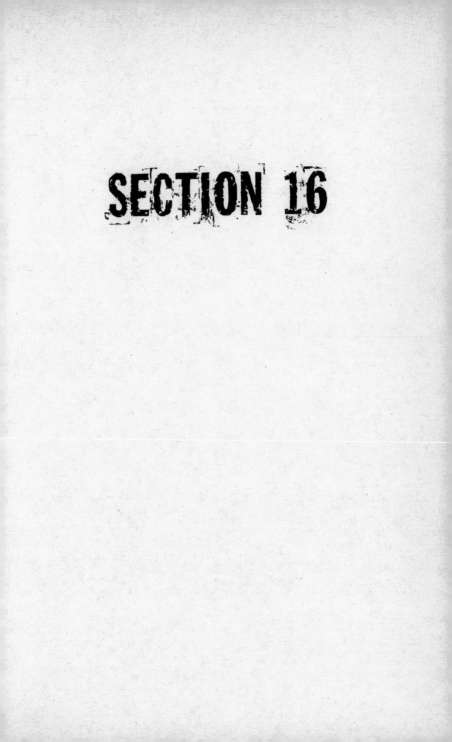

SECTION 16

THERAPY

Drumming Is Good For You...

Drum kits look great. People stare at them. There's nothing quite like the majesty of a drum kit, fully set up and waiting for its drummer. Whether fully lit on a stage or simply set up in a recording studio or living room, it is pure temptation. The drums themselves might be made in maple or birch, finished in oyster pearl, acrylic see-through, jet black or even green sparkle (like my DW). The gleaming stands and hardware could be gold, chrome or silver and the cymbals – Zildjian, Paiste, Sabian or any other make – always shine majestically, as if highlighting the whole spectacle.

Even when people can hear someone playing the drums on their own in another room, the urge is to go and take a look. Mark Laff, from punk band Generation X, told me about a recording session back in the 1970s.

We're recording the drum track to 'King Rocker' for the TV programme *Tiswas* in a small studio, which is part of the

Birmingham ATV television studios complex. It's just the engineer and me listening to the guide through my headphones. It's the fourth take and I'm desperate to get the track in the can as we've only got the studio for a short while. So I'm thrashing away, head down and concentrating hard. Suddenly I get this weird feeling, as though someone's watching me.

I look up to see a grinning face peering through the window into the studio. I recognise the face immediately but can't place it. I'd know it anywhere, that wide smile with the irritating moustache. Then it clicks. It's Adam Chance from *Crossroads*. The soap actor had apparently overheard the sound of the drums and followed the scent to the studio out of pure curiosity.

In other words, drums are irresistible. People who don't play always want to, and people who do never stop unless they have to. Whether you're a drummer or not, the idea of bashing hell out of something so beautifully constructed for the purpose is always appealing. It allows you to release energy. And it's different from running or swimming. There's something magical about the therapeutic effect playing the drums can have at any level. Sometimes, drumming can actually save your life...

ORGANISED CHAOS

It's 6pm and I'm seated behind a somewhat unusual drum kit in a large refectory. The kit is bright yellow, the hardware is like nothing I've ever seen in a drum shop and the cymbals are a combination of circular metal plates, some with specially drilled holes for restoration purposes. I've been asked to try the kit out. In front of me are about 20 rows of empty chairs, enough for around 100 people. A few guys are milling around.

A kindly looking gentleman offers to accompany me on bass for a brief jam session. I'm glad of this because I don't like doing solos on my own. I'm not very good at them. We get into a mid-pace funk/rock groove and I make use of the whole kit, putting in some favourite fills that I'm confident about. Afterwards there is generous applause from the other musicians who are hanging around.

The kit actually sounds great and the positioning is just how I like it. The cymbals aren't at all bad either, although there is one that makes an odd, tinny noise. But the standard of the drum kit is not the point. The fact that there is one here at all is impressive. Why? Because I'm playing the drums in Ford open prison in Sussex, near Brighton. The kit I'm playing belongs to lifer Steve Birnie, aka Jock, who is drumming this evening in a gig put on for some of the other inmates.

It's all part of a rehabilitation programme, led by Billy Bragg, called Jail Guitar Doors – a charity which aims to provide instruments, mainly guitars, in prisons to inspire inmates to learn and achieve. I've just finished interviewing Steve, who started playing drums when he was in Wormwood Scrubs. I didn't dwell too much on what exactly happened but he mentioned that his incarceration was the result of an unfortunate incident outside the nightclub where he'd been DJing. He's just turned 36 and he's due out of Ford in January 2010.

My dad is a jazz drummer and always wanted me to play. He

was a welder for a Scottish engineering firm Loblaw Drews and made his first drum kit himself. When I was about nine he used to sit me on his knee during the break when he was playing gigs in local hotel bars and introduce me as 'the smallest drummer in the world' and we'd have a go at playing 'I'm the King of the Swingers'. I never really took to it, though. I went on to become a DJ on the London club scene. And that meant drugs, dealing and all sorts. It was later termed as my 'chaotic lifestyle'. That's putting it mildly. And it was that lifestyle that led to me being banged up.

I started a three-year sentence, which was then extended because of a confused medical assessment, which claimed I had 'psychopathic tendencies'. This meant I now had 'lifer' status and was due to serve a further ten years in prison. On entering Wormwood Scrubs for the first time, I was told to put my chaotic lifestyle behind me: 'No more music, no more DJing!'

So I was facing not three but 13 years behind bars and I just didn't know how I was going to handle it. One day, on an exercise break, I was walking past the Scrubs music room and spied a drum kit set up at the back. Something clicked. I knew I had to do something to get me through the stretch without turning to drugs and I'd found it. It turned out the kit had been donated to the prison by a charity. I requested permission to use the room at certain times and, based on what my dad had showed me, taught myself to play the drums.

That has also led to me becoming the music man here at Ford and the resident house DJ on evenings like this. Since spotting that kit all those years ago, drumming and music have been my life. Without that, I really don't know how I'd have coped. Recently I had another medical assessment and I have been certified as mentally sound. I have officially lost whatever 'psychopathic tendencies' I had nearly 13 years ago. I'm leaving here for good next January, sane and drug free and I can tell you that's thanks to drumming.

Well, any drummer will tell you that playing the drums is therapeutic. But the irony is that although Steve was told on entering Wormwood Scrubs to leave music and DJing behind, it is precisely those things that have enabled him to find a pathway out of prison, clean and sober.

Steve also tells me that the yellow drums in use tonight were provided by the charity, but the cymbals were virtually unplayable and the stands and hardware have been cobbled together from old garden rubbish. 'Just like my dad's first drum set, this has been put together by a welder. Dad still plays and parties just like he used to. He's 67 and perfectly fit.'

After our interview, Steve gestures to his kit and the aforementioned five-minute jam takes place. A while later Steve has a bash. He plays some great jazz solo stuff and I notice the look of sheer joy on his face as his licks get faster and louder. I decide to stay for the show. At six o'clock inmates start to file in and after about ten minutes the seating area is pretty full. Steve is playing some atmospheric music on the decks beside the drums to set the mood. I watch several short sets by prison bands, interspersed by some good-natured banter with the audience until it's time for Steve's band. He gets onto the kit as the others plug in their guitars. He's obviously made a name for himself in this place as he's cheered from the start. The band play a mixture of rock 'n' roll standards and the audience love it, in particular the house favourite, 'Jailhouse Rock'.

As the last song finishes to roars of appreciation from a hundred or so inmates, Steve looks as if he's in the nearest place you can get to heaven in a prison. The conditions of his release for probation? Not to return to a chaotic lifestyle.

THE BRIXTON BASH

OK, so drumming didn't necessarily save Steve's life, but it stopped him deteriorating into a life of drugs in prison and that can, in some cases, lead to an early demise. Andy Theakstone, from the popular indie/emo fusion band Get Cape. Wear Cape. Fly, discovered that not only does playing the drums in prison have a therapeutic effect, simply talking about drums seems to lift the spirits.

Sam Duckworth [the main man behind Get Cape. Wear Cape. Fly] and myself had been invited to join Billy Bragg at a small show at Brixton prison for some of the inmates as part of Jail Guitar Doors. It was the first time I had been to prison. I have to say it was daunting and most inmates were pretty intimidating. The show was an informal gig at a small chapel in the middle of the prison. Around 30 inmates had been invited as a reward for good behaviour and because of their interest in music. Billy started the proceedings and took to the small stage. He is a charming man and pretty much won the crowd over.

That's kind of handy, really. Despite the aforementioned

good behaviour, and regardless of how it may have manifested itself, it would be reasonable to assume that immersing oneself amongst a load of incarcerated hard men might carry with it a certain element of risk.

Soon it was our turn to play. Sam and I hadn't planned much and certainly weren't about to try and do any classic Bob Marley covers like Billy had done; he could pull that off but we couldn't. Sam had decided we should play some tracks from the Get Cape. Wear Cape. Fly debut album, but stripped down. I had a snare, set of hats and some brushes, so it was very laid back. I really didn't expect much response but more than anything I hoped we wouldn't get any abuse! Luckily for us, it went pretty well. I'm not sure if anyone had heard of Get Cape, but I reckon we made a few new fans!

But what really surprised me was that te inmates I spoke to all seemed really interested in the drums. We ended up chatting about snares, cymbals, different musical styles and my favourite drummers (Jeff Porcaro, Brad Wilk, Gadd, Rich, Purdey etc). Some of the guys had also written some amazing songs. Good stories, honest and from the heart… It was a strange day and one I will never forget.

In recent years music and songwriting in general have formed a popular and important part in all kinds of therapy, including the rehabilitation of prison inmates, thanks particularly to initiatives like Jail Guitar Doors. But what is also interesting is that the art of drumming should reach such a high profile and take on such significance among people who need a lifeline.

But you don't have to be in prison to discover that drumming can become your reason for being somewhere.

MIRROR IN THE BATHROOM

The year: 1965. The place: somewhere above the Atlantic Ocean. A young teenager looks at himself in the mirror, which hangs in the tiny toilet at the rear of a passenger plane. Three hours before, he and his younger sister had waved goodbye to their mum and dad at the airport on St Kitts Island in the Caribbean. A sad moment for all concerned as, having saved every penny to achieve their plan, his folks had sent their children away to find their fortune, to make a better life for themselves.

Their destination? Great Britain, The place where music had only recently become pop. The Beatles and the Stones had been knocking solo singers off the No 1 spot for a couple of years and the hippy movement was only a couple of years away. The years to come would bring glam, bubblegum, teeny bop, reggae, progressive rock, psychedelic, disco, punk and shortly after that... a 2-Tone ska revival.

The mirror reflects the young, nervous face of someone who wonders what could possibly lie ahead for himself and his sister. The land of plenty to which they have been despatched may have been perceived to be full of opportunity, but it was not without its problems: economic, political, social. And young as he was, he knew this. You didn't just go to England and walk into a career or even a job. He hadn't a clue what he was going to do. He was, in fact, travelling on a wing and a prayer...

The year: 1966. The place: Birmingham, England. Sir Alf

Ramsey's team have just won the World Cup. The mood is jubilant. The Beatles' 'Yellow Submarine' is in the charts and the Summer of Love is just around the corner. A young black factory worker sweats in the mid-morning heat. He's busy working with large circular pieces of metal. Then the factory siren goes off and it's time for the morning tea break. The worker downs tools, but instead of going for a tea and a smoke, he starts to bash out rhythms on sheets of metal. A crowd gathers to watch. He's good. Very good. But they're all used to it. He does it at every opportunity – tea breaks, lunch times or just when he's bored and the boss isn't around. They think he's a bit nuts really but, hey, this guy's got talent. And it's not often you get entertained like that in a kettle factory.

The year: 1981. The place: a music festival in the US. A drummer checks his hair and make up in the mirror back stage. He's just about to play the drums in front of 70,000 people. He and his fellow band mates have just arrived by helicopter. The band has become one of the world's top ska-influenced bands, touring with people like The Specials, The Clash, Talking Heads and The Pretenders.

The year: 2007. The place: The Jazz Café in Camden, London. I'm sitting at the upstairs bar in the band's private enclosure, next to the man whose life's journey had taken him from that airport in St Kitts to the kettle factory in Birmingham and years later (via helicopter) to that festival in the US.

He's about to go on stage again. His name is Everett Morton and he's the drummer with The Beat. He tells me that he wasn't a drummer when he left his home in the Caribbean all those years ago. In fact, he hadn't a clue what he could do.

He just happened to end up working in a kettle factory, beating out rhythms on metal sheets out of boredom. Then he realised he had talent and started getting into the Birmingham music scene, rehearsing with various bands.

Eventually Everett was introduced to The Beat, a newly formed, multi-racial, ska-influenced group who happily embraced the sophistication of his polyrhythmic drumming and went on to be enormously successful. Since then there have been splits, reunions of sorts and lulls between further reunions. Nowadays Everett loves playing more than ever, but he's still amazed that all this has happened.

The Beat are headlining tonight. The heavily ska-influenced 2-Tone label (owned by Jerry Dammers of The Specials and which gave them their first hit) underwent a revival some years ago and their popularity has soared again. The place is hot and heaving in the venue below. Everett finishes his beer and goes backstage to get ready. As I wait for the band to start I'm wondering about this fate business.

The fact is, out of all the factories in existence in the '60s, Everett Morton happened to be given a job in one that made kettles, where he could bash out rhythms on hollow sheets of metal. What if it had been a sewing machine factory? Or a place that made outboard motors?

As The Beat open the set with their biggest hit, 'Mirror in the Bathroom', I can see the absolute joy and conviction on the drummer's face as he puts everything he has into his playing. And I know there is no place in the world he would rather be.

There are many drummers who really should be in this book,

but some are sadly no longer with us. One such legend, and some would say a legend among legends, is the great Buddy Rich from Brooklyn, New York. From playing the spoons reasonably well at the age of one, he went on to become the second highest paid child entertainer in the world (the first being Jack Coogan) and eventually the biggest name in jazz drumming ever. And he was completely self-taught.

Rich's sense of rhythm was so acute that he needed no instruction. In fact, he claimed that it would simply get in the way. This unique sharpness was noted by Rick Buckler of The Jam when he saw him play in London. Rich, it should be added at this point, was also a man who pulled no punches verbally...

I have always disliked setting up, breaking down, storing and lugging half a dozen drum and accessory cases around from gig to gig. So I was impressed with Buddy Rich when I saw him play at the Albert Hall. He had a small four-piece kit, but he made it sound huge. The place was full of drummers, and every eye was on Buddy throughout the show.

Halfway through one number he stopped, turned around and demanded that one of the brass section behind him take off his shoes, as he was tapping his foot out of time. I glanced around the hall and several of the audience were also nervously taking off their shoes, so as not to risk attracting the attention of Buddy.

There are more than 40 great drummers in this book, and my profound thanks go to all of them for being part of it. My thanks also to those who put me in touch with them (see the credit list – it's longer than a pair of drumsticks). There are dozens more notoriously great players who haven't made it into this book. Drummers, like other musicians, are very busy people a lot of the time.

And, of course, I had to stop somewhere and eventually I ran out of time. I'd like to leave you with a short piece which takes us back to where this all started, my local boozer...

OUTRO

White haired, rotund and with the air of one who has seen a good deal of the world, the drummer of The Northside Jazz Band plays with a light finesse that makes the whole business seem effortless. All of his 85 years are packed into his well-earned nonchalance as he stares out of the pub window for most of the band's set. Yet every stroke, every fill is executed with exactly the right touch. It is an expertise that can only be acquired through years of playing and more importantly, a love of the music itself. Sometimes, just for fun, he wears an old tin army hat on stage.

He has been playing in this particular pub, The Horns in Watford, every Sunday lunchtime for the past eight years. His wife, a white-haired, frail lady in her 80s, was his roadie. She would carry in his drums, one by one, with a dedication that would not allow her to accept help from anyone. She did this because he has a bad hip and cannot lift anything, and because she loved him more than anything else in the world. She passed away a couple of years ago, but he plays on every Sunday because that is what she would have wanted.

After The Northside Jazz Band have finished their set, I bring my own drum kit into the pub for a gig later on that afternoon. The old drummer calls me over. He needs some help getting to the toilet and takes my arm. He does have a stick but that's no good on its own as his hip has got worse. As we make our way slowly to the loo, over 30 years between us, he tells me he's still waiting for an operation, which will give him a new lease of life.

A great many people have an idea that drummers are a bit mad. Maybe so, but when I watch the white-haired old gentleman with his tin hat on, staring out of the window as he plays on stage in The Horns, I reckon there's probably no saner person on the planet. And his name?

Rocket Ron.